ARRIVEDERCI S

ARRIVEDERCI SWANSEA

How a Third Division reject became a Serie A superstar

MARIO RISOLI

MAINSTREAM
PUBLISHING

EDINBURGH AND LONDON

'MY HEAD IS AS
STRONG AS THE
MARBLE OF CARRARA.'

GIORGIO CHINAGLIA

First published in Great Britain in 2000 by
MAINSTREAM PUBLISHING COMPANY (EDINBURGH) LTD
7 Albany Street
Edinburgh EH1 3UG

ISBN 1 84018 283 0

A catalogue record for this book is available from the British Library

Typeset in Berkeley Book
Printed and bound in Great Britain by Creative Print and Design Wales

CONTENTS

ACKNOWLEDGEMENTS

I AM GRATEFUL to those, too numerous to mention by name, who have helped me with this project. I would like to thank those former players and officials who knew Chinaglia and have contributed to this book. They gave generously of their time and their memories. I am also indebted to the following who helped me with photographs – Dave Evans of the *South Wales Evening Post*, Alan Jones, Gary Owen, John Roberts and Terry Stevens.

I also want to thank David Farmer who provided me with useful statistics, Gordon Daniels who put me in touch with so many of Chinaglia's Swansea Town colleagues, and the staff at Swansea Central Library for their patient assistance.

The support offered by my father, Saverio, was invaluable. As always my wife, Catherine, provided endless encouragement.

ARRIVEDERCI SWANSEA

FOREWORD

I FIRST LEARNT of Giorgio Chinaglia when I was a teenager. My father often told the story of how a young Italian player, discarded by Swansea Town, went on to become one of the world's greatest strikers, helping Lazio win the Italian championship. Like many Italians living in Cardiff, my dad spent most of his bachelor nights in the restaurant run by Chinaglia's father. He remembered a young Giorgio bowling up with his girlfriends and demanding a steak sandwich. He also recounted the contents of a letter he had written to the Italian football newspaper, *Corriere della Sera*, suggesting the then unknown Giorgio Chinaglia should be allowed to play in Italy (because his registration was with the English FA, Chinaglia was classed as a foreigner by his compatriots). My father was, and still is, very proud of the fact that the letter was printed.

Chinaglia's story has always fascinated me. I could never comprehend how a forward deemed good enough to play for Italy in a World Cup and who was, in the early 1970s, among the world's best-paid footballers, had once been on the books of little Swansea Town. It was genuine rags-to-riches stuff, yet in Britain only a small band of people – die-hard Swansea supporters, a few Italian immigrants living in South Wales and a handful of journalists – are aware of Chinaglia's triumph after rejection. I hope that will now change.

ARRIVEDERCI SWANSEA

PROLOGUE

MAY 12, 1974. The penultimate Sunday in the 1973–74 *Serie A* championship. The sky is clear and the temperature is well into the '80s. Inside the Stadio Olimpico, the concrete bowl stadium shared by Rome's two football clubs, Roma and Lazio, there are 80,000 people, all hoping to see Lazio's first ever title triumph.

The men from Rome face Foggia, a team from southern Italy fighting to avoid relegation. If Lazio win they will be crowned champions of Italy, regardless of what second-placed Juventus do in their home match against Fiorentina. It is two points for a win, and Lazio have a three-point cushion over the Turin club.

The Olimpico is a sea of sky blue, Lazio's colours. Scarves, flags and banners cover the vast open-air stadium. The supporters had been arriving three and a half hours before the 3 p.m. kick-off. Outside, the roads leading to the Olimpico are jammed with traffic.

In the Lazio dressing-room the atmosphere is tense. The players, 90 minutes from making history, are visibly nervous but their coach, Tommaso Maestrelli, wearing his favourite tweed jacket, is serenity personified. As they prepare to enter the tunnel that leads onto the pitch Maestrelli, as he does before every game, shouts at each one of his players '*Chi non lotta! Chi non lotta!*– Who is not fighting! Who is not fighting!'

The first half is frustrating for Lazio. Foggia, desperate for a point, build an iron wall in front of their goalkeeper, Raffaele Trentini, and the home side play only in sporadic bursts. It is Foggia who launch the first serious attack, after nine minutes. Giuseppe Pavone's shot fools Felice Pulici, the Lazio goalkeeper dressed in all black. The ball is heading for the empty net, but Luciano Re Ceccioni turns it away for a corner before it crosses the line. The supporters breath a collective sigh of relief, but within seconds their anxiety returns. The huge electric scoreboard reveals all to those who have not heard the news via the thousands of transistor radios scattered throughout the stadium. Juventus are leading Fiorentina thanks to a goal from Pietro Anastasi.

Lazio take 24 minutes to test the Foggia goal. Re Ceccioni finds Vincenzo D'Amico and his fierce shot hits the post. But the visitors appear to have tamed the *Serie A* leaders and Foggia coach Lauro Toneatto is winning the tactical battle with Maestrelli. Foggia's four–man midfield suffocates the creative Lazio players such as Re Ceccioni and Mario Frustalupi, while Franco Nanni and D'Amico are both playing below par. Toneatto's masterstroke, however, is pinning two defenders on Lazio's giant forward, Giorgio Chinaglia, who is so often his side's match winner. Stopper Novilio Bruschini and sweeper Giovanni Pirazzini follow Chinaglia like two pickpockets stalking their victim through the city's narrow streets.

Francesco Panzino blows his whistle for half-time and the disconsolate Lazio players return to their dressing-room. The plan had been to kill off Foggia in the first 45 minutes and they had failed. Maestrelli tries to calm them. 'You are doing nothing wrong,' he tells them. 'Carry on playing the way you are playing and you will win the game.' They return for the second half but within five minutes they lose their inspirational right-back, Luigi Martini, with a shoulder injury. Five minutes after he leaves the field Foggia hit the crossbar.

But on the hour Lazio get their break. In front of the Curva Nord, the north section of the stadium where Lazio's hard-core *tifosi* gather, Renzo Garlaschelli, Chinaglia's dark partner in the Lazio attack, crosses. Francesco Scorsa, the man marking Garlaschelli, jumps to intercept the cross but loses his balance. His arm blatantly touches the ball and Panzino has no hesitation in pointing to the penalty spot. Scorsa, not a first-team regular, pleads his innocence. He screams at Panzino that the handball was not intentional. His team-mates surround the Calabrian referee and it takes a full three minutes to restore order.

Lazio's penalty-taker is Chinaglia. He places the ball on the white circle and walks back a few yards for his run-up. The supporters in the Curva Nord, unable to watch, turn away, as does Re Cecconi. He puts his arms on his hips and looks at Felici Pulici in the opposite goal.

Chinaglia strides towards the ball and hits it with his famous right foot. Trentini dives to his left, but he has guessed wrong. Chinaglia picks the right corner. The ball zips along the grass and into the net. The Olimpico erupts and chants of *campione! campione!* – champions! champions! – can be heard from the terraces. Chinaglia starts to run towards the bench. He always hugs Maestrelli after scoring, but this time it will be difficult to reach him. As he heads for Maestrelli, he is stopped by Nanni and before he can wriggle free, the rest of his colleagues are around him. After a couple of minutes normality returns and as Foggia are about to re-start, Chinaglia jogs to the touchline to embrace his coach.

The last quarter of an hour seems an eternity. Lazio are reduced to ten men. The tension has taken its toll on Garlaschelli and he is sent off for a retaliatory foul on full-back Rodolfo Cimenti. Foggia attack Pulici's goal as Lazio cling to their lead. Making up for the numerical disadvantage, Chinaglia chases every ball across the pitch. Lazio fans, many of them wearing T-shirts with Chinaglia's face printed on them, make their way to the gates at the edge of the pitch, preparing for the invasion.

According to the scoreboard Juventus are winning 3–1, Anastasi scoring all three goals. But the result is irrelevant. Lazio's defence, the best in *Serie A*, holds firm. Panzino blows the final whistle and thousands of supporters flood onto the pitch. In the Curva Nord blue balloons are released into the humid Roman air and a huge banner which reads *Grazie Maestrelli* – Thank you, Maestrelli – unfolds. In the middle of the pitch a fan plants a placard containing the names of all the Lazio players into the ground. Lazio's captain Giuseppe Wilson, his shirt ripped off his back, is carried aloft by the *tifosi*.

Chinaglia, exhausted, puts his arm around Maestrelli. That penalty not only won his team the championship but ensured he finished the season as top scorer – *capocannoniere* – with 24 goals. That day in May 1996 when he was given away by Swansea Town of the Third Division seems a distant memory.

ARRIVEDERCI SWANSEA

CHAPTER ONE

CARRARA IS A charming town in Tuscany, north-west Italy. In the province of Massa, it is 55 miles from Florence, the region's major city, and lies at the foot of the Apuan Alps amidst olive groves and vineyards. The town grew around the world's most important marble quarries. At the peak of production, in the nineteenth century, Carrara boasted some 400 quarries all providing marble of different quality and colours. Michelangelo was a regular visitor to the town, supervising work at the mines.

It was here, in the marble capital of Italy, that Giorgio Chinaglia was born, on 24 January 1947. Chinaglia's mother, Giovanna, like most Italian women just after the Second World War, gave birth not in a hospital but in the family's home, helped by a midwife who was paid two thousand lire – the equivalent of just under one pound. He was the elder of two children. Rita, his sister, was born three years later. Chinaglia's mother was from Carrara but his father, Mario, was from Portogruaro, a small town near Venice. A trainee cook in the Army, he had moved to Carrara during the war.

The Italian economy was devastated by the war. Unemployment was rife and the once-prosperous Carrara, which saw much of its 80,000 population employed in the marble industry, was badly affected. Chinaglia's father was among the jobless and his family lived mainly on bread and *zabaglione*, a frugal mix of egg, sugar and coffee, which became the staple diet in most households after the war.

Desperate for work, Mario Chinaglia, along with hundreds of his fellow countrymen, emigrated to the UK in 1955, to take up a post in the iron and steel industry. A severe labour shortage had affected the heavy industries and the British factories turned to Italy for labour. Job placements were advertised in Italian towns and cities, at the local *ufficio di collocamento* – employment agency.

At the office in Carrara, Chinaglia's father saw an advert by Guest, Keen and Nettlefolds in Cardiff, South Wales. The steelworks had opened a second furnace and needed men to cool the ovens. The pay was six pounds and five shillings a week plus one pound for bed and breakfast. Mario signed up with Carrara-born Andrea Delnero. The pair left Italy in October 1955. 'I remember when we arrived at the railway station in Cardiff it was a miserable day,' recalls Delnero, who shared a terraced house with the late Mario Chinaglia in the Welsh city. 'We had nothing except the watches on our wrists and the gold chains round our necks. It had been a turbulent trip. On the boat from Calais to Dover we were all being sick. We thought we were going to die in the English Channel.'

Mario Chinaglia had left behind his young family who were being looked after by his wife's mother. He promised, once he had earned enough money, to bring them over to Cardiff. It took him a year before he was able to return to Italy to collect them. The family's journey from Carrara to Cardiff took two days. A train to Genoa, then another train to Milan and on to Calais. From there, the ferry to Folkestone, then another train to London, and from London a fifth train journey to the Welsh city.

Giorgio, nine, and Rita, six, arrived at their new home in the early hours of the morning. With no buses or taxis operating at that time, they were driven from Cardiff Central Station to their new address in the back of a Post Office van. Mario had rented a solitary room in a house in Richmond Road, a terrace of large Victorian properties close to the city centre. 'It wasn't a good impact,' Chinaglia recalls, when asked about moving from Carrara to Cardiff. 'It was always snowing and raining.' The worst feeling in the world, he said, was water seeping through the insole of his shoe.

The Chinaglias stayed in Richmond Road – they had crammed in a double bed for the parents and a put-up bed for each child – until 1960 when they could afford larger accommodation. They moved to a two-bedroom apartment in Talbot Street, again near the centre, but across the other side of the city. Having left the hot, gruelling conditions of Guest, Keen and Nettlefolds, Mario Chinaglia was working as a chef at The Gourmet, a city-centre restaurant. Not long after moving into Talbot Street the Chinaglias invited Andrea Delnero to live with them. Delnero recalls, 'I used to see Giovanna on my way to work. She would say "Why you no come and live here?" I said I was happy where I was. Then one day Mario asked me. "There's plenty of room," he said. So I moved in. They had two rooms but the main bedroom was very big. Rita moved in there with her parents and I stayed in the other room with Giorgio.'

And so began his friendship with *Giorgione* – little George. With the boy's parents working long and unsociable hours – Giovanna was a kitchen assistant at a popular steak bar called The Continental – Delnero became a surrogate uncle to the future Lazio star. 'If I was free in the afternoon we would go to Sophia Gardens and play football,' says Delnero. A popular recreation area in Cardiff, Sophia Gardens was a series of playing fields a few minutes' walk from Talbot Street. 'I used to take Giorgio and Rita. One day there were these Hungarians there. They had come over because of the Uprising. We played football with them and pretended it was Italy versus Hungary. They were very kind. Because Rita was in goal they didn't shoot hard. They tried to walk the ball in.'

It was Delnero who taught Chinaglia how to kick a ball, against the wall of their Talbot Street home. He would also watch him playing for his school, shouting advice from the touch-line. 'When Giorgio came home from school,' adds Delnero, 'he used to go into the kitchen. It was a nice big kitchen. You know what he would do? He would put the table aside and play football with his sister. I played with him as well because he always won against his sister.'

Delnero, still employed at the steelworks at the time, often played cards in Café 41 in Tiger Bay, a bustling, multi-racial (but now demolished) area in Cardiff's docklands. His card games were sometimes interrupted by Chinaglia who wanted him among the spectators for a football match. 'I remember one time he was playing for a team from the Ely estate called Ely Bridge. They used to ask him to play because he was good. His father would never be there because he was working so he wanted me to come because I would shout *tiro!* – shoot! – when he was near the penalty area,' recalls Delnero.

'I used to tell him, "There's only a little boy in goal, so shoot." He would score two or three goals at a time because he would take shots. Another time he came to the café and said to me, "I have to play in Newport for the school in the cup." I was playing cards but I had to leave everything there to go and watch him. His team won 2–0 and Giorgio scored both goals.'

Chinaglia's first school was St Peter's Primary, the nearest Catholic junior school to Richmond Road. At first, he could not speak or understand a word of English but by the time he left the school, when he was 12, he could converse with his schoolmates, albeit with a heavy Italian accent. 'In a month,' he later recalled, 'I learned the language, which was pretty good.'

Chinaglia quickly became anglicised and on one occasion, when he was 14 years old, his newly acquired identity enraged his father, a patriotic Italian. The date was 24 May 1961. England had just beaten Italy 3–2 in a friendly in Rome. Gerry Hitchens scored twice and Jimmy Greaves hit the winner four minutes from time. Chinaglia admitted to his father that he had been cheering for England. '*Traditore!*' – you traitor! – screamed his father. '*Sei Italiano, non Inglese!*' – You are Italian, not English! – and chased after his son to give him a hiding. The teenager fled to the lavatory and locked himself inside. His father banged on the door shouting '*Sei Italiano o Inglese?*' – Are you Italian or English? – while his mother cried, '*No, no, non picchiarlo!*' –

No, no, don't hit him! After four hours, when his father had calmed down, the teenager finally unlocked the lavatory door.

At St Peter's he was introduced to Wales's national game, rugby. 'I played rugby because there was no football. I didn't play football until secondary school,' says Chinaglia. 'Rugby was OK. It helped me a lot in my career. I used to go home aching on a Saturday.' The sport was alien to him since rugby was unheard of in Italy, but he was in Wales now and the young Italian – tall and well-built for his age – was seen as an ideal second-row forward by his rugby-obsessed sports teachers.

'I remember playing against Giorgio in the Cardiff Under-11s League,' recalls Kevin Lyons, a former pupil of Herbert Thompson Primary School. 'He wore a scrum cap, I'll never forget that. He was the only boy wearing one. We all wondered where he got it from because only a couple of players wore them at senior level. He obviously felt he needed it for protection.

'He was tall, big and had this cap on. You couldn't really miss him,' adds Lyons. 'He didn't seem to fancy rugby too much. When they threw the ball to him in the lineout he got rid of it straight away. I don't think he liked the physical side of it, the buffeting, the rough and tumble. But he always tried his best, even though he didn't enjoy it.'

After St Peter's, Chinaglia went to Lady Mary, a Catholic secondary school in Cyncoed, an affluent suburb in the north of the city. At that time Lady Mary, made up of two separate buildings, was split in half – the boys' school and the girls'. Both schools had their own headteachers. Jack Sharkey was in charge of the male half and Sister Mary Christopher the female half. They also had their own playgrounds and interaction between male and female pupils was strictly forbidden, punishable by the cane.

'Giorgio arrived just before me. I joined Lady Mary in year two and he was in year three,' says Salvatore Amodeo, another Italian immigrant in Cardiff. Like Chinaglia, Amodeo was a Tuscan, from Grosseto. And like Chinaglia, his family emigrated to Britain to find work. Two of his brothers were in the steelworks while his father was employed at a textiles factory. 'Even though I was younger than him there was an affinity between us because we were both Italian,' says Amodeo. 'When I first started school there were a few lads picking on me. Giorgio came along with two of his friends and sorted them out, nothing nasty. It was like being initiated into the school Mafia! Everyone left me alone after that. Giorgio was looking after me because I was Italian. It was his two friends who really did it. They were seen as "hard" boys.'

Pupils at Lady Mary were streamed into four classes – A, B, C and R – depending on ability. The A class contained the brightest boys, those tipped as potential O-level candidates. Chinaglia was put into the B class. 'He was not a star pupil in the academic sense,' recalls Amodeo. 'He wasn't thick. I just don't think he was interested in the academic side of school. He didn't like school work. His only love was football.'

Lady Mary attracted Catholic children from across the city. It was a strict school. Male pupils were caned *en masse* if nobody owned up to any wrongdoing. Boys were also slapped across the side of the head if they were guilty of any insolent behaviour. 'Giorgio wasn't naughty, he was just mischievous,' says Amodeo. 'He tended to mix with who I would call the semi-troublemakers. They used to smoke in the toilets, shout at girls, do a bit of mitching now and again, things like that.'

Not only were male pupils barred from any contact with the girls during school hours, they were also prohibited from talking to them in the school drive, as they entered and left the buildings. One of the nuns used to hide behind the bike shed, which was situated on a blind bend along the drive, to catch any pupil disobeying this rule. Another former pupil of Lady Mary, Tommy Broad, who became good friends with Chinaglia, says, 'Giorgio was in our group. There were eight or ten of us and we all sat at the back, right the way through school. We were OK at our studies but we never knuckled down. There was the studious half of the class and the rebellious half, and we were part of the rebellious half. Giorgio was bright, he had it all upstairs. You couldn't fiddle him for a penny, but I think his attitude was "I'm going to play football so I don't have to pass my exams".'

Chinaglia admits he did not enjoy his days at Lady Mary. 'Treatment at school wasn't so good. I came from an ethnic background and it was very difficult. There were two sections, one was the ethnics, the other was the Welsh, and there used to be fights. That was normal. The teachers were useless. They went through the job they had to do, those six hours, and that was it. To be honest, I can't remember the name of one teacher. That tells you the whole story.'

As with many youngsters who aspire to become footballers, Chinaglia showed little interest in studying. As Broad recalls, 'He would give any excuse to get out of lessons. For instance, one of the teachers bought this old Vanguard car and he was looking for boys to rub it down to the bare metal. It was a project for this teacher and it was going to take three months. Giorgio was one of the volunteers. While he was rubbing it down one of the staff caught him smoking. Giorgio was lying on the back seat rubbing down the back door so he didn't see him coming.'

Chinaglia watched enviously as his friends in metalwork escaped doing any academic work. 'In the metalwork room there was this storage area used to keep tools,' adds Broad. 'We used to say we were going inside to get something and not come back out. Giorgio was in woodwork and they didn't have a place where they could hide. Giorgio used to come over to the metalwork area so he could go into this room as well but he used to get caught. "You're not in here, Chinaglia, get out!" the teacher used to shout at him.'

The Italian schoolboy proved a useful member of the class when it came to English. The teacher was Tom Keeley, who had been an RAF pilot during the Second World War. When asked about his favourite subject, namely aviation, Keeley would spend the entire lesson talking about it. 'We'd say to Giorgio, "Ask him a question about the war" because if he did we wouldn't have to do any work,' says Joe Smart, one of Chinaglia's closest friends during his Lady Mary days. 'Keeley would start going, "When I was flying over France . . . " If we asked him a question he would think we were up to something so we got Giorgio to ask. Keeley had a soft spot for Giorgio because he couldn't speak English very well.' Broad also recalls those English lessons. 'Giorgio would ask him something like "What's the difference between an aerodrome and an airfield?" That was it, lesson over. We could spend the next half hour looking out of the window.'

Some teachers had a nickname for most pupils. Chinaglia was known as 'the wop', an epithet that would be unacceptable today. 'Giorgio was one of the daredevils, always sat at the back throwing bits of paper about,' says Selwyn Parsons, another of Chinaglia's former classmates. 'He was always winding this one boy up. This lad was a bit deaf and he always sat in front of Giorgio in class. One day Giorgio threw some paper at one of the teachers when he had his back turned. The teacher thought it was this boy in front of Giorgio. This lad never used to do anything wrong but he was told to leave the class. "I'm not going," he told the teacher. The two of them ended up fighting on the floor and we all doubled-up laughing.'

Salvatore Amodeo also found himself in trouble while following Chinaglia on one of his escapades. 'Giorgio and some of his friends had found this underground tunnel which connected the boys' school with the girls' school but we got caught. We were called in to see Mr Sharkey and I remember him telling me, "Amodeo, I never thought you'd be involved with these boys!"'

Chinaglia was regularly late for school, arriving 10 or 15 minutes after the morning bell. 'We caught the bus to school,' says Tommy Broad. 'Giorgio got on a couple of stops after me. We had to be in at 9.15 a.m. and if we caught the 8.55 a.m. bus we got in right on time. But if we got the 9.05 a.m. bus we were obviously going to be late. If you were late, you needed an excuse. What we used to do was send this one boy in ahead of us – his name was Richard Thompson – and while he was giving the teacher his excuse, me and Giorgio would try and sneak in. It wasn't easy because Giorgio was so big.'

According to Broad, they usually arrived late four days out of five. 'Giorgio used to blame the bus and say it was late. If the teacher said other boys caught the same bus but managed to get in on time, Giorgio would say he caught the wrong bus, had to get off and then wait for the right one. When we were late I used to ask him what excuse he was going to give and he'd say, "What did I give yesterday?"'

Poor punctuality was not Chinaglia's only shortcoming. He also used to fall asleep during lessons. While he was at Lady Mary his father switched restaurants, moving from The Gourmet to the Cellar Bar, another city-centre establishment. At nights Chinaglia could be found working there with his father, to earn some extra pocket money. 'He always had plenty of money. Never short of a few bob was Giorgio,' says Selwyn Parsons. 'He always had a fiver in his pocket and five pounds in those days was a lot of money.' In the restaurant Chinaglia washed dishes, made coffees and occasionally waited on tables. But the late finishes – sometimes he did not get to bed until 2 a.m. – inevitably took their toll on the youngster.

'He would come into school half asleep,' recalls Broad. 'I remember him in the science class. There were these big wooden benches screwed to the floor and Giorgio would put his feet up on them, lean back on his stool and say, "Tell me when someone's coming." Then he'd fall asleep. The teacher used to wake him by kicking his stool. Giorgio used to bring girlie magazines into school and we'd look at them at the back of the class,' adds Broad. 'One time, in the science lesson, the teacher was coming towards us so he stuffed them inside this cupboard. I said to him, "You'd better get them at break otherwise someone is going to have a nasty surprise if they open a cupboard to get a Bunsen burner." He went back at break and told the teacher he'd lost his comb and could he look for it. He got the mags, shoved them up his jumper and left.'

During his five years at Lady Mary, Chinaglia was part of an inseparable trio which included Joe Smart and Lawrence Howes. 'Giorgio used to get us into a lot of trouble,' remembers Smart. 'He'd clown around in class and because he didn't speak that much English, me and Lawrence got the blame. We had a few canings because of Giorgio.' Smart recalls one incident during a science lesson. 'He threw something at the teacher, I can't remember what it was. The teacher was writing on the blackboard when he did it and he turned round and threw the chalk at us. "You three out here!" He caned me and Lawrence even though we hadn't done anything. "It's always one of you three and if I cane all of you I'll get the right one," said the teacher.'

According to Smart, if Chinaglia was caught up in any trouble he would simply say, 'I don't understand' with a strong Italian accent. 'He liked to go for the sympathy vote and he turned the accent on when he wanted to, especially when there was something wrong!' says Smart. 'He didn't get up to anything malicious, just tomfoolery. He was boisterous like a lot of boys that age. He liked to be the centre of attention.'

Some teachers were driven to despair by the excitable Tuscan. On one occasion his mother was summoned to the headmaster's office after he pulled the music teacher's wig off. Another of Chinaglia's targets was the blonde, attractive art teacher, Geraldine Mahoney. 'She caught Giorgio and I making lustful gestures at her once,' recalls Tommy Broad. 'She went mad and I remember Giorgio saying to her, "It's not my fault you are beautiful!" When he walked past her he would make these deep sighs.'

One day Chinaglia went too far. As Selwyn Parsons recalls, 'The whole class got the cane because Giorgio made her cry. He was always saying "Phwoooor, Miss Mahoney" and "Oooooh, yeeeess" when we were in her class. One time he made some wisecrack about her figure as she was handing out books. She started shouting, "I've had enough! I've had enough!" We all had to go to the hall for the cane. When we went back into the class you could hear a pin drop it was so quiet.'

The biggest altercation involved the burly rugby teacher, Frank Callus. As soon as Chinaglia arrived at Lady Mary he was approached by Callus who once played prop for a Cardiff rugby side, Old Illtydians. He wanted him for the school rugby team but Chinaglia was only interested in playing football. 'One day he came home from school,' says Andrea Delnero, 'and I said to him, "You play football today?" He said no. "Why not?" "Because I have to play rugby," he said. So I told him, "You go back there and say my dad wants me to play football, and if I don't play football he'll come to the school."'

But Callus was determined that Chinaglia, the biggest boy in the first year, should play rugby. With his physique and natural athleticism, he would have made an ideal centre, flanker or winger. 'He played rugby for St Peter's and the sports master there told me, "You've got a good lad coming up" so of course I grabbed him,' says Callus. 'I thought to myself, "I'll make a rugby player out of you, mate." He was quite speedy and I thought of him as a centre, but Giorgio had other ideas. So did his father.' Since his son's pleas not to play rugby were being ignored, Mario Chinaglia paid a visit to the headmaster, Mr Sharkey. Callus recalls, 'My head sent for me and I went to his room. Mr Chinaglia was there. I said Lady Mary was primarily a rugby school, that Giorgio was a big boy and I could use him on the rugby field. His father said, "Italians don't play rugby!" His father was quite adamant so I had to give way.'

The row between rugby and football surfaced again two years later, when Chinaglia was in the third year and was cajoled by his friends into playing in an inter-house match. There were four houses at Lady Mary – St Patrick's, St Illtyd's, St Cadoc's and St Teilo's – and Chinaglia played for St Patrick's. He caught Callus's eye.

'We talked him into playing and he had a stormer of a match,' recalls Tommy Broad. 'A couple of weeks later, Callus, who was now a form tutor, said, "Chinaglia, you're playing rugby." Giorgio said, "No chance." That was on a Thursday or Friday. On the Monday, Callus said, "There's training tomorrow, I want you there, Chinaglia." Giorgio said he wasn't going, he was playing football. This went on and on. Then Giorgio stood up. He must have been eight inches taller than Callus. Callus poked him, Giorgio poked him back. Callus pushed him, Giorgio pushed him back.' The teacher then marched Chinaglia into a room where sports gear such as hurdles and javelins were stored, and shut the door. 'We could hear all this scuffling,' says Broad. 'The door opened, Giorgio came out and went through one door and out the other. Callus came out. He was covered in dust and his hair was all over the place. He had this swelling under his eye. He told me and a couple of other boys to go and find Giorgio but we couldn't.

'Later in the day Giorgio's father brought him back to school. Giorgio said his dad had clipped him around the ear because he had hit someone who was smaller than him!' That was the last day

Chinaglia was badgered about not playing rugby. 'Callus got off Giorgio's back after that,' adds Broad. 'He didn't pressurise him anymore. Callus was the type of person who respected you if you gave it back.'

Football was very much a second-class sport at Lady Mary. 'The school football coach, John Williams, was a hell of a nice man,' says Salvatore Amodeo, 'but he didn't have a clue about coaching football. There was no enthusiasm for football at the time. The rugby department had lots of balls, all the flagsticks and Callus had an assistant to help him. With football it was all amateurish and haphazard. I was surprised. When I came to Wales, I thought, "This is where John Charles comes from, they must all play like John Charles." But I soon found out that wasn't the case.' Joe Smart puts it more succinctly: 'Rugby was seen as a man's game. Football was for poofs.'

The school's best athletes were coerced into playing rugby. They may have made better football players and they may have preferred to play football, but if Callus wanted them for rugby, they played rugby. Chinaglia was the only one who rebelled.

'When you arrived at Lady Mary you were expected to play rugby,' says Kevin Lyons, who also attended Lady Mary. 'That was the game everyone was expected to play. I felt if you weren't good enough at rugby then you could play football. That was the culture at Lady Mary.' Lyons, who later played cricket for Glamorgan, was one of the many pupils too scared to challenge Callus. 'Looking back, I was frightened by the teacher. I played for Cardiff Schools at rugby but I would have made the Cardiff Schools soccer team, no doubt about it.

'Callus was a strong, dominant bloke and rugby was his game. He wanted Lady Mary to be at the forefront of Cardiff rugby. It was, "I'm picking you for rugby and I want you there." He was a big, broad, powerful man. He had a fearsome look about him, didn't smile a great deal. I was scared of him. Giorgio used to ask me why I wasn't playing football. He would shrug his shoulders and throw his hands in the air. "You play what you want to play." But there was this threat with Callus – if you don't play rugby, I'll make your life a misery. Teachers weren't like they are today. In those days you had the cane or the belt. He taught Geography and I was shit-scared of him. He banged my head against the blackboard once because I didn't know where Porth [a town in the Rhondda Valley] was.'

Chinaglia was regularly ribbed about playing the round-ball game as opposed to the oval-ball one, but he showed no desire to switch allegiances. 'We used to call him chicken because he didn't want to play rugby,' says Tommy Broad. 'He used to say, "I don't want a broken nose like you." Another one of his favourites was, "All ugly people play rugby."'

Football was the one aspect of the curriculum at which Chinaglia excelled. He was the school's outstanding player, as Salvatore Amodeo remembers. 'He was on a different wavelength. When he had the ball, even in midfield, he would beat a man and then lay off a pass into space but there would never be anyone there. "What are you doing? You should have been there!" he would shout. He was way ahead of anyone else in that respect.'

Joe Smart describes Chinaglia's selfishness on the football field. 'If he had the ball that was it, he wouldn't pass it. Once he had the ball he had to score, it didn't matter if there were 15 or 20 blokes in front of him – he had to score.'

After finishing school Chinaglia would return home, grab his football and then round up his friends to play in Sophia Gardens. 'I went to a different school to Giorgio and when I came home I would find him outside my house waiting for me,' recalls Piero Caramella, who lived a few doors away from Chinaglia. 'He'd have the ball in his hand and he'd say, "Come on, let's go!" and he'd collect some of the local boys for a kick around. He used to organise everything during the game – "You do that, you do this" – he was a real leader.'

For a few weeks after the summer holidays, there would be no sign of Chinaglia at Lady Mary. He was always the last to return, as Frank Callus recalls. 'He always disappeared for a month or so every year because he went back to Italy to play for Young Juventus in these football tournaments. He would return to school with reams of newspaper cuttings which he presented to me along with medals that he'd won. I don't understand Italian but I looked at the cuttings and would see his name mentioned plenty of times, so he obviously did well.'

Callus adds, 'His soccer skills were superlative but he didn't have the modesty to go with his ability. All the lads thought he was a good player and Giorgio knew he was a good player. They'd tell him he was good, and he'd say he was good himself. He'd also say they weren't very good and this didn't always go down too well! Whether it was with teachers in school or managers when he was a professional footballer, he was frank and open with his views. He had no respect for authority. He was outspoken, he had an arrogance about him. But he was a nice lad in his own way. He liked to come and talk to you. It was always about himself though! I remember before he went to Italy in the summer his Italian accent wasn't that heavy but when he came back it was very much to the fore. It would take a few weeks for him to settle back to being a Welsh boy again.'

One aspect of football Chinaglia did not enjoy was training. Later, when on Swansea Town's books, he would gain a reputation for being a poor trainer: not trying, turning up late, sometimes not even turning up at all. 'He used to mess about,' says Salvatore Amodeo. 'He was very erratic. He enjoyed playing football but he found running back and forth very boring. He'd get told off so many times for messing about. "Shinaglia!" – that's how the teachers would pronounce his name – "Get back to the changing-room!"' Another of Lady Mary's Italian contingent, Antonio Leto, a Sicilian who was in the same year as Chinaglia but in the R stream, recalls, 'He loved football, kicking the ball around. If he missed a goal he would fall on his knees and cry. We used to play on a full-size pitch, two against two, and he would run from one penalty area to the other to score a goal.'

Kevin Lyons vividly remembers Chinaglia in impromptu games in the school playground. The Italian was in a class of his own, displaying skills that were unfamiliar to his Welsh peers. 'He was just too good for them. He'd stop and juggle the ball,' says Lyons. 'Some of the other kids would just stand and watch him, which was quite unusual. He entertained us, knocking the ball onto his knee and head. I think Giorgio enjoyed the attention.'

Although he had won his battle to play football, Chinaglia could not force the sports teachers to nominate him for the Cardiff Schools trial, held during the summer holidays. As he began his final year at Lady Mary, and despite his goalscoring feats for the school team, he was not involved in Cardiff Schools Under-15 team. But then he had the good fortune to play for Lady Mary against St Patrick's, another Roman Catholic school from the working-class Grangetown area of the city. Their coach was Terry Stevens, one of the three Cardiff Schools selectors. Impressed by the Italian striker, he invited him to join the Cardiff squad.

Lady Mary, that bastion of rugby, now had one of its pupils in the city's schoolboy football team.

CHAPTER TWO

IN THE CARDIFF SCHOOLS' TEAM, Chinaglia – at nearly six foot tall, with a powerful physique and an Italian accent – was something of a curiosity. David Summerhayes, a wing-half in that side, recalls seeing the Italian for the first time. 'He was a frightening figure, like a freak. He was a big lad with these broad shoulders. At schoolboy level, if you were big you were half-way there. To me, he didn't have much skill but he got away with it because he was so big.'

Chinaglia's height made an impression on all his team-mates. 'He was towering over us,' says Roy Palfrey, who played wing-half.

Doug Curtin, the outside-left, recalls, 'I was only small and when we walked onto the pitch he'd be head and shoulders above me. He was 14 but he looked 18. To talk to him, I had to look up. He had this gruff voice as well.'

The team trained every Tuesday and Thursday evening, at Coronation Park, a small patch of inner-city greenery behind a bus depot and close to Ninian Park, the home of Cardiff City. The parkland was distinguished by a derelict double-decker bus which acted as a makeshift changing-room for the players and shelter for spectators in bad weather. 'I remember Giorgio turning up,' says Curtin. 'He used to wear an overcoat with the collars turned up. He didn't seem to have a neck. He was always hunched up, like a gangster.'

Because of Lady Mary's rugby bias, Chinaglia did not appear for Cardiff Schools until he was 14, playing in the Under-15 side. Several members of that team already knew him. One of them, Steve Derrett, first met him at junior school in a baseball match. Chinaglia was playing for St Peter's while Derrett was playing for Greenway Road, a school in east Cardiff, an area dominated by council estates built in the 1950s and '60s. 'He couldn't speak any English and he was chasing everyone with the bat because they were taking the mick out of him. He was quite volatile, even then.'

Derrett also encountered Chinaglia at secondary school. 'I went to a school called Cae Castell and I played against him when we met Lady Mary. I was half-back, he was centre-forward. I wouldn't have called him an outstanding player in those days, not someone you'd think would be special enough to play for Italy. It's a miracle what happened to him.'

Phil Raybauld, the right-half in that side, was another Cae Castell pupil. He first encountered Chinaglia when they were 13, on a cold and frosty Saturday morning at Pontcanna Fields, where Lady Mary faced Cae Castell for a school match. As the Cae Castell minibus pulled into the car park just before the 10 a.m. kick-off, Raybauld noticed a crowd of children on the pitch. In the middle was Chinaglia the showman performing a series of ball-tricks. 'He was flicking the ball up onto his knee and volleying it into the goal and these little kids went scurrying after the ball to give it back to him. Giorgio was spotless. He was wearing all-white and it was sparkling white. He was terribly well-groomed. His shorts were gleaming, his boots were polished and had white laces. You'd look at him and think, "Crikey, Moses!" Most of the boys I played with had come off council estates but you looked at Giorgio and you knew he came from a good home. He had black hair which was slick and curly. He cut an image which was quite different.'

Chinaglia was clearly doted on by his parents, who subsidised the spanking-new football kit and supplied steak sandwiches when their son showed up at the restaurant. To his mother, Giovanna, her son was always 'il mi' Giorgio' (my George) – and such worship must have contributed to Chinaglia's self-belief. Reg Litten, who played inside-forward for Cardiff Schools, first met the Italian when he was 12, via a mutual friend. 'We used to go to the park and play football together. Even then I thought to myself, "Crumbs, this boy's useful!" He gave me the impression he was very confident. If you're confident that goes a long way to making an impact in sport because you believe in yourself.'

John Seaford, who played football with Chinaglia during the summer holidays, remembers him as a good-looking and athletic boy with an Italian accent, who struggled to speak English. Seaford was surprised the Lady Mary pupil had not broken into the Cardiff Schools side earlier. On a Saturday night he would look through the pink pages of his father's *Football Echo*, the local sports paper which came out early Saturday evening. Virtually every week Chinaglia was mentioned. 'All the school results were in there so if you scored for your school your name would be in the paper, which was quite a big thing for us kids,' explains Seaford. 'My mum used to cut them out because my brother and I played. Giorgio would always be in there. Lady Mary would win 6–0 and you'd see "Chinaglia (six)". People used to talk about him and say, "Why isn't he in the Cardiff Schools' side?"'

The answer, of course, was that he attended a rugby-biased school which frowned on football. To play for Cardiff Schools a player had to count on the support of his sports master who would nominate pupils for the summer trial. Rugby schools such as Lady Mary rarely put forward pupils for football. 'All the Roman Catholic schools tended to be rugby-orientated,' explains Paul Crocker, who was centre-half in the Cardiff Schools team and would join Swansea Town at the same time as Chinaglia. 'I played at all levels – Under-11s, Under-12s, Under-13s, Under-14s – and Giorgio wasn't in any of those teams. He wasn't on the scene at all.'

Phil Raybauld remembers playing against Chinaglia and describes him as a prima donna. 'He was a glitzy sort of player. He tried all the flashy things but he wasn't a grafter. He didn't like hard work. We always knew when we played Lady Mary that if we took him out of the game we had a chance. But he scored some spectacular goals, unbelievably spectacular goals for a 13 or 14 year old. I do recall him scoring long-range goals. He'd pick the ball up in the middle of the park, usually from someone who had won the ball for him, and he would shoot with great power and accuracy. Once he had the ball there was only one focus – the goal. But we knew if we stopped the ball going to him he wouldn't be a danger because he never went looking for it.

'He was difficult to get the ball off. He was very strong from the waist down and his close control was immaculate. He would take people on, go over the ball with one foot and take it with another. He was incredibly confident, not afraid to try things. He really did have tremendous ball control. He could bring it down on his chest, his thigh, his feet. He'd try delicate chips, volleys, half-volleys. We hadn't seen anything like it before. He was class and if you were standing on the line watching him you would have been impressed.'

As well as the fancy tricks and long-range shooting, Chinaglia liked to chat with the other players. 'He'd talk right through a game,' adds Raybauld. 'He'd talk to us, the opposition. "How's it going?" He was friendly, very pally. If you were standing next to him he'd start talking to you. Looking back, I wouldn't say he was very competitive. We beat Lady Mary a few times and I got the impression that it didn't matter to Giorgio as long as he scored.'

Even though he was a prolific goalscorer for Lady Mary, Chinaglia was unable to command a regular place in the Cardiff Schools first team. 'A lad called Gordon Roberts was keeping him out of the side,' says Richie Morgan, inside-forward in the team. 'Giorgio was a squad player really. He never quite made it.' Roberts, the centre-forward, was a prolific goalscorer, the city's school sprint champion and the star of the schoolboy side. He was playing for the Under-15s when he was only 13 and, before he left school, was snapped up by First Division giants Wolves, the Division One champions three years earlier. 'Giorgio was unlucky,' adds Morgan. 'A year later and maybe he would have been a first-choice player. But that year Gordon was there and he was extremely strong and quick for his age. He was the boy everyone thought would go on and do things.'

Despite their rivalry, Roberts and Chinaglia became good friends. 'We went out together quite a few times,' recalls Roberts. 'He was – how can I say it? – familiar with one or two nightspots. We were 14 going on 15 and Giorgio would knock on the club's door. A shutter would open and he'd say, "It's Giorgio." In we went! It was a surprise to me because we were so young, I mean, we were only kids. These must have been his Italian contacts. Giorgio seemed to know everybody at every place.' The pair would hit the town on Friday or Saturday nights – no drinking, just dancing and eyeing the girls. 'We were young and it was the '60s,' smiles Roberts. 'We were lads being lads. The scene was brilliant then.'

Chinaglia was known as Snagglepuss by his team-mates, after the American cartoon character. Some of his teenage affectations left the other boys bemused. Roberts says, 'For training and matches he sometimes brought a hanger with him, so he could put his clothes on it. He used to spend a lot of time on his hair as well. Shampoo was the in-thing and he'd use shampoo whereas we would use soap and water. We'd be having a shower and all of a sudden there was this smell – it was his shampoo.' Chinaglia also made sure he had the latest gear. 'If it was in fashion, Giorgio would have it,' adds Roberts. 'He had the best socks. Newcastle had these socks at the time, they were white with black squares at the top, and Giorgio had a pair of those. On the schoolboy scene he did have a reputation for being an arrogant so-and-so. Some of the other teams didn't like him – "You know who plays for Cardiff, that Italian bloke" – but I knew him away from football and we were good pals. He wanted your companionship. He genuinely wanted to be your friend.'

Phil Raybauld was also struck by Chinaglia's taste in fashion. 'We never knew about design at that age but Giorgio was a cool dresser. He wore a lot of white. He always wore white socks and black shoes. He liked black drainpipe trousers and winkle-picker shoes. Winkle-pickers and chisels were fashionable in those days and Giorgio was a winkle-picker man. We used to wear donkey jackets and duffel coats but he had an overcoat and it was stylish and well-kept. If I remember rightly, it was handed down to him from his father. He was obviously a boy who was doted on.'

Since Gordon Roberts was the untouchable centre-forward, the selectors – Terry Stevens, Joe Cross and Bob Ord – picked Chinaglia as a right-winger. 'They wanted to fit Giorgio in somewhere and because he had a good right foot that's where they put him,' recalls Doug Curtin. The wing, though, was not the ideal position for Chinaglia. 'He was good on the ball but he was a bit flashy, chipping it here and chipping it there. He wasn't doing what a winger should do, beating his man and getting the ball across,' says Curtin. 'He used to do these overhead-kicks on the wing! With his back to goal he'd flick the ball up and all of a sudden he'd overhead kick it into the middle of the pitch. We'd watch in awe because we couldn't do things like that. He used to do a lot of overhead kicks.'

As right-half, Raybauld worked with Chinaglia on the right side of the pitch. 'It wasn't the best position for him. He wasn't a very fast player. He needed space to get going and on the wing there was always someone who closed you down. No, he never struck me as a natural winger. I used to put balls past the full-back. He liked those but he didn't always get there.'

Roberts remembers one match where Chinaglia upstaged him. Cardiff Schools were playing the team from Welshpool, a small town in rural mid Wales. 'It was a Welsh Cup game. If my memory serves me right it was a semi-final. I was playing up front and Giorgio was on the wing. I'd recently signed for Wolves and Stan Cullis, who was Wolves' manager at the time, came over from Wolverhampton to watch me, to see what he was getting. Anyway, I was having a terrible match so they stuck me onto the right wing and moved Giorgio to the centre-forward position. He had a very good game and scored a goal. After the match I went to see Mr Cullis. I was very concerned because I'd played badly and he did mention Giorgio, saying he was interested in him.'

The class of 1961–62 was one of the most impressive in Cardiff

Schools' history. Four of that team played for Wales Schools – Paul Crocker, Richie Morgan, Reg Litten and Gordon Roberts. 'We were a cracking side,' says Reg Litten. 'We had a good squad of players and if somebody dropped out there was another who could come in and do a good job. Giorgio arrived and started pushing for a place. There were quite a few players battling for positions and you had to work hard for your place.'

Chinaglia was picked for the squad despite not being put forward for the Under-15s trial, held in the summer break at Llandaff Fields, a large area of parkland in north Cardiff used for rugby and football games on the weekends. 'What would happen,' explains Morgan, 'was that your school would nominate you for the trial. About 30 or 40 kids would turn up and the selectors, who were all teachers, would organise a first trial, a second trial and a final trial. They'd look at all the players and pull off the ones they thought were good enough. It was a process of elimination.'

Rugby-loving Lady Mary may not have nominated Chinaglia but the selectors, who could not ignore his goalscoring exploits for the school's football team, picked him. 'He was a centre-forward pushing hard for my position,' says Gordon Roberts. 'When he was playing for Lady Mary I was aware of his cockiness. He was very confident and seemed to want to get on in football. I found him very friendly.'

Opinions on Chinaglia's ability as a schoolboy vary. Some, such as Richie Morgan, were unimpressed. 'He was good on the ball, moaned and didn't want to work. He was a nice boy – always had a smile and he wanted to be everyone's mate – but he didn't do much on the field and he wasn't the bravest of players.'

John Seaford agrees. 'I always got the impression that if he didn't get his own way it affected his game. He didn't like it if someone roughed him up. He didn't like any physical contact.'

Steve Derrett was another who thought Chinaglia would fail to make the grade. 'He was big, quite fast but pretty volatile. He'd moan about everything. No, I wouldn't have classed him as a good player in those days.'

But others marvelled at his exquisite ball control. 'Giorgio was good. He had that arrogance,' says Roy Palfrey. 'At that age we never had close control but he did. Fair-dos to him, he could play football.'

Roberts, too, admired the Italian's ball skills. 'I was all blood and thunder, chasing everything. That's what they wanted in those days but Giorgio could pull the ball down and do unusual things with it. He had ball control and a great first touch. He was cheeky and arrogant but not in a nasty way.'

Chinaglia was only ever a fringe player for Cardiff Schools. According to Palfrey, that was not just down to the competition from Roberts. 'The selectors didn't like individualism and Giorgio was a bit individualistic. In those days it was all about teamwork – pass, pass, pass. It was very regimental. But Giorgio would want to run and run, and they didn't go for that. To be honest, Giorgio was a bit too good. Cardiff wasn't ready for him.'

Frank Callus offers another reason as to why he played so few games for Cardiff. 'He came up with some ripe language on one occasion. I forget who they were playing but he let the whole side down.' Callus knew about this use of foul language because a complaint was made to Lady Mary. 'I know the teachers involved in the game took a very dim view of it. Giorgio learnt English but he also learnt bad English as well. He blotted his copybook pretty badly and I'm sure he never played for the team again. Even though he was outstandingly good, they were not prepared to put up with his attitude and the bad impression he gave other schools. He used foul language while representing Cardiff and his arrogance upset his opposite numbers. It left a bad odour. It came back to the school and we felt very upset by it. The head saw Giorgio and as far as I know he never played for Cardiff Schools again.'

The schoolboys from Cardiff were viewed as 'the posh lot' by the other teams in Wales. Not only were they representing the Welsh capital city but they also wore white silk shorts. In poor mining towns in the Valleys, such as Aberdare and Merthyr Tydfil, this was quite a talking point. 'The way Giorgio played,' says Roberts, explaining his view of why the Lady Mary pupil was such a peripheral figure, 'was not him being arrogant or selfish, that was just him. It was the Italian style. We didn't know about it back then.' Chinaglia struggled even to get a run on the right-wing. Two other youngsters, John Seaford and Bobby Day, were also vying for that position. 'In British football, skill came low down the list,' continues Roberts. 'First it was blood and thunder, then you had to have guts, then speed. Skill came fourth. Giorgio insisted on playing his style and that's why he didn't make too much of an impression. He'd be brilliant now. With defenders not being able to kick you when you've got your back to goal, Giorgio would run riot. Really, he came along too early.'

Terry Stevens admits Chinaglia did not easily fit into the team. 'He was the type who would juggle with the ball when I wanted him to be more positive. He could do tricks with the ball but in those days football was more direct,' explains Stevens. 'Also, because he was tall and gangly he could be easily hustled off the ball. He wasn't an automatic choice because we had better players, simple as that.' When he did play – and occasionally, when Roberts was absent, he took his favourite role of centre-forward – he did score goals. Years later, Chinaglia insisted he scored eight goals in one Under-15 match and ten in another, although his former team-mates have no recollection of such feats.

The 1961–62 season saw Cardiff Schools reach the semi-final of the English Schools Shield, the flagship competition. Never before had a Cardiff team progressed so far. (The city was to wait until 2000 for a side to equal that achievement.) Cardiff played these games at Ninian Park. First they beat East London Schools 2–1 in Cardiff. Next came Hull Schools at Boothferry Park in Hull. After drawing 2–2 in front of a 500-strong crowd, they won the replay 2–1 in Cardiff. In the last eight, they met Coventry Schools at Highfield Road in Coventry. In a floodlit game, played in ankle-deep mud, Cardiff won 2–1.

They were drawn to face Liverpool Schools at Ninian Park in the semi-finals. Chinaglia had not played in any of the previous Shield games but was picked to play the game against Liverpool on the right wing. It was a disaster. Liverpool walloped Chinaglia and his team-mates 6–0. 'We really thought we were going to win that game,' says Doug Curtin. 'We'd come all that way and we had a home draw as well. It was all over after 20 minutes, they were either two or three goals up by then. They were so much better than us, just different class. The selectors were elated we got that far, but they were so dejected after the match. We genuinely thought we had a chance. We had four boys playing for Wales – that was a lot for one team. But Liverpool were something else. You don't normally get beaten in a semi-final 6–0. Normally it's by one goal or two, not six.'

Terry Stevens adds, 'It was played under floodlights and I think that played havoc with our goalkeeper. We were two down in no time.'

After the game Chinaglia and the rest of the team sat inside the vast Ninian Park dressing-room, shattered. The selectors were speechless and some of the players were close to tears. 'We were a good side but that day we were absolutely useless,' says Gordon Roberts. 'Whatever we tried we couldn't upset them and it was one-way traffic. But give credit to Liverpool, they had some skilful lads.'

Reg Litten believes an outbreak of smallpox in Cardiff was to blame for the heavy defeat. 'We were on the crest of a wave when the smallpox came along. Everybody was having injections. People's arms were swelling up and games were cancelled. We had such a long lay-off from football. Several weeks went by without us playing a game. I'm not saying we would have beaten Liverpool but I think we would have played a far more competitive game.'

The team's progress in the English Schools Shield had caught the attention of clubs across the UK. Normally, the scouts watching Cardiff Under-15 matches were working for Cardiff City, Swansea Town and the two Bristol clubs, City and Rovers. But now there were different faces at Ninian Park, scouts working for clubs in London, the Midlands, the North-West and even Yorkshire. Many youngsters in that Under-15 side were given trials by professional clubs. Roberts went to Wolves, Morgan and Litten both went to Leeds United, Palfrey went to London to try his luck with Crystal Palace, Seaford to Bolton Wanderers and Crocker to Swansea.

As for Chinaglia, he was offered a trial by Cardiff City, who had just been relegated from Division One. To the amazement of his peers, he refused to go. Recalls Frank Callus, 'The scouts asked him to go for a trial and he said, "If you want to see me I'm playing against Wrexham. Come and see me play then!" Chinaglia detested the idea of trials. "The word trial tells you everything," he once said. "Either you're good or you're not good."'

When no other clubs showed an interest, his defiance vanished and Chinaglia did go for a trial with City. The Bluebirds turned him down. 'I thought something was wrong when they took me on and not Giorgio,' says Salvatore Amodeo, 'because he was a much better player. I always felt it was crazy.' Of the rejection, Chinaglia remarked, 'You are never a prophet in your own town. At Cardiff you had to be good in the air and useless with the feet.' However, Callus believes he was not taken on 'because his outspokenness didn't go down well there, either'.

Swansea Town, Cardiff's great rivals, were looking for a young striker. Paul Crocker, recently offered trials by the Swans, was paid a visit by Walter Robbins, the club's coach. Recalls Crocker, 'He said they were looking for a striker and were interested in Gordon Roberts, but Gordon was spoken-for by Wolves. He asked if there was anyone else we could recommend and I'm sure that's how Giorgio's name was brought up.'

Robbins decided to watch Chinaglia in action and the match he picked was Cardiff Schools against Wrexham Schools, at Coronation Park. Chinaglia remembers, 'Walter saw things in me, he saw the skill.' Cardiff won 3–0, with Chinaglia scoring all three goals. Robbins, a former Cardiff City and Wales outside-left, invited him to the Vetch Field to look at the club's set-up. 'One lunch time during pre-season training,' recalled John Irvine, who was in charge of Swansea's 'A' team, the third team, 'Walter turned to me and said, "Can you do anything about Chinaglia?" When I saw that he was six foot tall I said I would have him in my team right away. Even then, at 15, he had a man's physique.'

After a month's trial – 'which I hated' – Chinaglia was offered apprentice-professional terms. 'He was a very capable player,' says Terry Stevens. 'He played a few games for us and didn't let us down. I wasn't surprised Swansea took him.'

For Chinaglia it was the beginning of four unhappy years in Dylan Thomas's hometown.

CHAPTER THREE

IN THE SUMMER OF 1962, Swansea Town had a well-established but unspectacular Division Two side. The Swans won promotion from Division Three (South) in 1949 and had been in the Second Division ever since, sometimes battling against relegation but usually enjoying relative comfort in mid-table.

Trevor Morris, the club's trilby-wearing manager, was in his fifth year at the Vetch Field when Chinaglia arrived. Morris, the son of a miner, was born in the rugby heartland of Carmarthenshire, in rural West Wales. A former wing-half with Cardiff City and Ipswich Town, his playing career was cut short while on leave from the RAF. He broke his leg on 'a cold, frosty day' in a wartime match for Cardiff against Bristol City.

During the Second World War, Morris served in Bomber Command as a pilot and flew more than 40 missions, leading a Lancaster squadron on D-Day and winning the Distinguished Flying Medal before returning to football in 1946 as Cardiff City's assistant secretary. Cardiff then had a First Division club and in 1954 Morris found himself promoted to manager – or secretary-manager to be precise – following the resignation of Cyril Spiers. But the Bluebirds struggled among the élite and they were relegated in 1957. 'They had got there by a fluke and the team was not strong enough to make a permanent place for itself in the premier division,' remarked Morris at the time.

In the summer of 1958, and after 19 years at Ninian Park, Morris announced his departure. He had agreed to become Swansea Town's general manager and signed a three-year contract. Morris effectively ran the club. Not only was he in charge of first-team matters, he was also responsible for administration, balancing the books, and buying and selling players. 'I don't know if he knew about soccer. He was more of a public relations person,' says Chinaglia of Morris.

Morris was never seen wearing a tracksuit at the Vetch, always a collar and tie. The hands-on coaching duties were left to former Welsh international Walter Robbins, who, in his youth, bore a striking resemblance to Hollywood star Errol Flynn. He was helped by Irishman Steve Leavy. Morris appeared more concerned with the day-to-day running of the club, especially the financial side, and worked closely with the club's newly appointed secretary, Gordon Daniels.

'We used to call Trevor Morris "the snake" because he was always licking his lips,' recalls Paul Crocker. 'And we called Gordon Daniels "the squirrel" because he was buck-toothed.'

The Swansea Town supporters viewed Morris with suspicion, a man more concerned with reducing the club's overdraft than producing a team which could win promotion to the First Division. Prior to Chinaglia's arrival, Morris had sold Swansea's best and most marketable players. First, inside-forward Ivor Allchurch – nicknamed Golden Boy – joined Newcastle United for £25,000. Then the club received a record £43,000 from Arsenal for the versatile Mel Charles, younger brother of Juventus star, John. Morris also accepted £25,000 from Middlesbrough for Welsh international centre-half Mel Nurse. Following Nurse's departure the city's evening newspaper, the *South Wales Evening Post*, was inundated with letters from angry supporters, one describing Morris, the war hero, as 'nothing more than a business manager for the board'.

When Chinaglia signed apprentice forms at the Vetch, the team had just finished third from bottom and escaped the dreaded drop by three points. It was a marked contrast to the previous season when the Swans finished a highly creditable seventh.

Since Chinaglia lived in Cardiff, Morris asked two of his other Cardiff-based players, Mike Hayes and Mal Gilligan, to pick up both Chinaglia and Crocker on their way to Swansea. Both Hayes and Gilligan owned cars – Hayes had a Sprite while Gilligan had a Morris Minor – and each morning they would make the hour-long trip on the winding, cross-country A48 to report for training at the Vetch, a ground located near the sea-front and a stone's throw from Swansea Prison.

Neither Hayes nor Gilligan was a fully-fledged first-team member. Both played regularly for Swansea in the Welsh League, a considerable step down from the Football Combination, which was where reserve teams usually played. The Swans had recently withdrawn from the Combination in one of Morris's money-saving schemes.

'We used to drive down on alternate weeks,' says Gilligan. 'One week I used to take them in my Morris Minor, the other week we used to go down with Mike in his little sports car.'

Hayes recalls, 'I had a call from Trevor Morris that this Giorgio Chinaglia was going to sign for the club and would I meet up with him and his parents to discuss taking him back and forth to Swansea. I didn't mind at all. In fact, he was good company because the A48 was a long haul.'

Chinaglia was no stranger to Gilligan. He recalls seeing the Italian playing football at Sophia Gardens. 'I used to practise shooting and crossing there with a fellow called Dilwyn John who became goalkeeper for Cardiff City. I used to see Giorgio playing football with little kids. They were only tots and he'd be dribbling around them – dribble, dribble, dribble. He'd get the ball straight from kick-off and he'd keep hold of it. Giorgio was a big lad for his age and there were these little kids trying to get the ball off him! He loved playing with youngsters, probably because he could have the whole game to himself. It was different when he came into the real world.'

Sophia Gardens, on the banks of the River Taff which divides Cardiff in half, was Chinaglia's favourite recreational haunt since it was only a couple of minutes' walk from the family home in Talbot Street. 'I remember trying to find Giorgio once,' says Hayes, who was several years older than his Italian team-mate. 'Trevor [Morris] wanted to get a message to him, I can't remember what it was about. I went to his house. His dad said he was out with his sister and that probably they were at Sophia Gardens. So I went there – my wife was with me – and I found Giorgio playing football with his sister. He was dribbling past her so she couldn't get the ball off him. I shouted over to him, "Giorgio!" He came over and said to me, "Why don't you just fuck off!" My wife was quite shocked. He was just embarrassed that we caught him showing off, but he did swear a lot for a youngster. I just got used to it.'

In 1963 the M4 had not reached Swansea. The journey west, on the A48, was a tortuous one, through the quaint county town of Cowbridge, then Bridgend and finally past the imposing towers of Port Talbot's steelworks. 'The old car took a hell of a hammering with Giorgio and Paul in the back,' says Gilligan. He remembers one journey in particular. 'We had a big argument once. We were coming back from Swansea and I was driving. Giorgio was in the back with Paul. The road was very icy and Giorgio started rocking from side to side. He was throwing the car around. It was only a little Morris. I said to him, "For Christ's sake, stop! You're gonna kill us all!" I think we got to Cowbridge before I saw a lay-by. I said to him, "Are you gonna stop?" He carried on rocking the car, so I stopped and said, "Out! We'll settle this outside!" We both got out and when he wasn't looking I jumped on him and got him in a grip. "Now look, it's my car and I'll go to the manager and say I'm not picking you up anymore. It could be the end of your career."' Chinaglia backed down and the remainder of the trip passed without incident. 'He was just being a teenager, I suppose,' says Gilligan.

Was it a bad fight? Crocker recalls, 'Put it this way, neither of them needed a blood transfusion. Their handbags might have been muddy, mind. We used to have arguments in the car but usually it was about favourite players. Giorgio was a fan of Bobby Charlton but we used to fancy Jimmy Greaves. Charlton was Giorgio's idol. At the ground he used to mess around pretending he was him. He used to run on his toes, like a marionette, shouting "Bobby Charlton!" every time he kicked the ball.'

Training at Swansea would start at 10 a.m., finishing shortly after midday. Hayes says, 'I lived in Canton, the same area of Cardiff as Giorgio. I'd call at his house at 8 a.m. and we'd get to the ground at 9.30 a.m. or 9.45 a.m. It was a good hour and a half to Swansea in those days. [On the M4 it takes only 40 minutes to reach Swansea from Cardiff.] Sometimes Giorgio couldn't get out of bed and I had to wait for him. I used to tell him, "I'll give you 15 minutes and that's your lot." Occasionally he'd keep me waiting 20 or 25 minutes. That was the longest. And then he'd come out of his house not having washed and his appearance wasn't at its best. He'd be changing in the back of the car.

'We always used to stop in Port Talbot on the way back,' continues Hayes. 'Giorgio had to go into Ferrari's cake shop for these big cream cakes. They were the biggest they had and he'd slowly eat them on the way back. Sometimes we'd stop for a pint but Giorgio was only interested in these cakes. He wasn't a drinker. He was just happy with a cream cake and a soft drink. Usually he'd drop off as well because he was a lazy so-and-so.'

The lifts with Hayes and Gilligan soon came to an end. Morris no longer wanted the pair commuting from Cardiff every day and ordered them to find digs in Swansea. For Chinaglia and Crocker, it would have to be the bus or train. However, they came up with another idea. 'I don't know if the management ever knew about it but we bought scooters,' explains Crocker. 'Giorgio always fancied himself on a scooter. We used to travel back and forth every day on these Lambretta scooters. We used to do a hundred miles every day and we'd bomb there and back.

'We didn't want the club to know about them because it wasn't allowed so we used to park them in the British Legion car park, which was round the corner from the Vetch. Then we'd walk to the ground. We used to give our helmets to the British Legion bloke with a couple of bob and he would look after them for us. I'm sure the club didn't know about it. I bought a new scooter. I'd just had an in-house loan from my grandmother. Giorgio acquired a second-hand one. His dad wasn't too pleased about it, I remember that. I don't think he wanted him to have a scooter. Even though he was a young man I think he wanted Giorgio to discuss it with him first, and Giorgio didn't.'

A footballer's apprenticeship lasted two years and when not training Chinaglia worked on the groundstaff. The jobs included sweeping the stands, wiping the seats, cleaning the dressing-rooms, working on the pitch and cleaning boots. 'Working in the boot-room was considered the best job because you were in the warm,' says Colin Park, who was goalkeeper in the Swansea 'A' team. 'Also the pros would give you their old boots if they got new ones.'

Chinaglia was assigned to sweeping the stands. 'That was all right because you had a chance of finding money, a pound note here and there,' continues Park. 'It was better than working outside on the pitch.' Menial and unrewarding as these jobs were, most trainees regarded them as part of a professional footballer's rites of passage. But the Italian resented doing these chores – 'I had to clean the stands, clean the boots of players who couldn't play, all that shit. Give me a break!' he remembers – and it soon became clear he had no intention of doing his fair share of work.

'We used to cover for him no end of times because he was always lying about,' recalls John Harries, an apprentice at the same time as Chinaglia. 'When he should have been cleaning the stands he'd be lying somewhere.' Harries, a right-back and a local lad, joined the Swans the previous year and had played for Wales Schools. 'He'd keep out of sight and hide in all sorts of places. He would just disappear and then we'd find him lying down. In the old "double-decker" stand at the Vetch, there was a room storing mattresses and mats which were used in training. Chinaglia was often to be found in there.

'With Trevor Morris, anybody who came from Cardiff had special treatment,' adds Harries. 'He thought it was a feather in his cap when he stole someone from Cardiff. That's how we Swansea boys felt, anyway. We were just numbers cleaning the ground. Giorgio got away with a bit more than us. He was a skiver but he got away with it. We'd clean three rows to his one and he was always trying to get out of his job. He used to say, "I've got to go and see someone." Yeah, sure. But you couldn't dislike him. He was a tidy fellow but a lazy bugger.'

Geoff Thomas, another groundstaff contemporary of Chinaglia's, adds, 'All he wanted to do was play football and he felt he couldn't do that if he was sweeping the stands. But you had to do those jobs when you were an apprentice.'

Dolly Phillips, who was in charge of the club's catering and who joined the Vetch Field staff in 1947 as a cleaner and tea lady, also remembers Chinaglia's lack of enthusiasm for groundstaff chores. 'He wouldn't do the jobs. Boys at that time had to help around the ground. The seats and stands had to be cleaned – you couldn't get any cleaners in Swansea to take that job on. I did have a couple of women once. They only worked a couple of days before they downed tools and said, "We're not doing this!" But Giorgio would never be around. He would hide in a place where they could never find him.'

On one occasion, Chinaglia demonstrated his petulance when Bert James, the club's elderly handyman, asked him to paint one of the stands. 'OK, I'll paint the stand,' he said, taking the pot of paint. He opened the tin and threw the contents against the stand. It is a story Chinaglia, who maintains he was at Swansea to play football and not to learn DIY, tells to this day.

Alan Wilkins, a midfielder in the Welsh League side and who became Chinaglia's best friend at the Vetch, described him as 'the laziest person on the groundstaff'. He adds, 'He was always saying he had to go and see somebody or he had to do some sort of errand. He'd also go to the toilet for an hour. He was never where the work was, skiving all the time. Maybe that was his upbringing. His mum and dad pampered him a little bit.'

One member of the coaching staff sympathised with Chinaglia – Bill

Edwards, the youth-team coach. 'I didn't agree with the groundstaff thing. You didn't get many groundstaff boys who wanted to work,' he explains. 'When you go to a football club you go because you want to become a footballer so why should you be painting stands and cutting grass? They were interested in becoming footballers, not interested in how high the grass was.'

There was one occasion, on the eve of an FA Cup game against Queen's Park Rangers at the Vetch, where Chinaglia was ordered to muck in with the rest of the apprentices. The winter of 1962–63 was harsh, with heavy snow falling in December and January. The third-round match against QPR in January was at risk of being postponed so the groundstaff boys were ordered to work through the night, thawing the frozen pitch with braziers. Used by councils, these were bins of hot coal with holes in them to release the heat. Once the grass had thawed, they had to cover it with sand to prevent waterlogging.

Rather than stay outside all night, Chinaglia ushered his colleagues to the warmth of the dressing-room and organised a card session. 'He liked a gamble,' says Bernard Morgans. 'Not for a lot, just a couple of shillings.' Every so often they would leave the dressing-room and move the braziers five yards. The game was saved and when a delighted Trevor Morris arrived at the ground later that morning he told the apprentices, 'Extra money in your wages at the end of the week!' The bonus turned out to be a solitary one pound. 'We'd been working all night and we were only given a pound,' says Morgans. 'That upset Giorgio a bit. He wasn't happy with a pound because he'd been working practically 24 hours. He felt a fiver would have been more fair.'

Chinaglia was a compulsive card-player, as John Hedges, at the time Swansea's chief scout, recalls. 'Giorgio loved to gamble and he was a good card-player. We used to travel to away matches on the train in those days and he'd bring a pack of cards with him. Him and Geoff Thomas, they were big gamblers. Trevor Morris stopped them gambling because it would affect their performance during games. If you lost twenty pounds playing cards you wouldn't play well, so Trevor banned them playing at the club. I remember Giorgio wasn't very happy about that.'

Pre-season training took place on playing fields belonging to a steel plant, Richard, Thomas and Baldwins (RTB), in Landore, north of Swansea. The club often used the company's sports facilities during the summer months. 'We did all the groundwork there and that was where I first met Giorgio,' explains Brian Thomas, a full-back who was knocking on the door of the first team. 'This is a true story about him. There's this canal which runs along RTB and in the first couple of weeks of pre-season we had to run on the path along the canal which went all the way to Neath, about five miles away, and then run back. I remember Giorgio collapsing on the way back. He absolutely collapsed – couldn't move. The boys in front got back and told Walter that this Italian boy was on the floor, laid out. Walter had to go and get him in a car. It was his first week of proper training and I think it was the shock of it all.'

Mal Gilligan recalls a similar story. 'It was either the first or second day of training and we were doing a run. Giorgio went out ahead of the established pros like Barrie Jones and Colin Webster who were superfit guys. Giorgio started running out in front. We tucked in at a nice pace but he shot ahead of everyone. It was the first few days so it was a bit hard but he was definitely showing off. Of course, the next day he's sitting down with blisters on these big feet and he couldn't train.'

During the season, the players trained every morning at the club's training ground at nearby Skewen, a football pitch circled by a dog track. The apprentices trained with the first-team players when there were no groundstaff jobs to be done. Otherwise they trained in the afternoon on their own. 'For instance, on a Monday morning the stands had to be swept so that had to be done first,' explains Geoff Thomas. 'Sometimes we'd be asked to help Bert out with some of his handyman jobs, like replacing broken glass or touching-up paint. Generally, we had to clean the ground.'

As an apprentice, Chinaglia occasionally angered the management. Tommy Jackson, another of the groundstaff boys, recalls, 'We were playing discus with this piece of stone by the East Entrance to the Vetch. Chinaglia wanted to join in. "I can do that!" He threw it from under his chin and he ended up smashing this lean-to that belonged to a house right next to the ground. We scattered to the four different corners of the Vetch!'

Geoff Thomas also remembers that incident. 'The whole lot just came crashing down. John Harries and myself fell on the floor laughing. I don't know if he did it deliberately. The lean-to was a fair distance from where we were playing so he must have intended it. We got a major bollocking and the club had to pay for the glass that was broken.'

Thomas recalls another incident, this time involving Syd Tucker, the club's elderly, bad-tempered groundsman. 'Syd worshipped the ground. We weren't allowed to train on the pitch, but in the afternoons we used to go back there and play on it. There would be five or six of us, including Giorgio. One day Syd caught us and started chasing us. But Syd was an old man and he pulled a muscle. He went down like a sack of potatoes. We thought he was acting but he wasn't and we got a real bollocking for that too.'

The frail Tucker, with his wellington boots, overalls and obsession with the pitch, became a target for the more mischievous players. Chinaglia, together with Alan Wilkins, relished playing practical jokes on him. 'They were crazy to Syd Tucker,' says Colin Webster, one of the senior pros when Chinaglia joined the Swans. 'They used to drive him absolutely nuts. How he didn't commit suicide I don't know! They used to tie his laces together when he was having a little sleep. They'd leave booby traps for him, positioning a tool so that when he moved it everything in his shed would collapse. They'd put water on his seat, silly things like that.

'They used to put seeds on the pitch as well. During pre-season they used to re-seed the Vetch. Giorgio and Alan would go into Woolworths and get these seeds and mix them with the grass seed. We'd have radishes coming through, cabbage, the lot! Syd would go, "What's this?" It would be lettuce. "What's that!" It would be beetroot. Syd would be shouting, "We've got to get this seed firm down here to sort this out!" But he soon found out it was Giorgio. Whenever something went wrong it was Giorgio. "Wait till I get my hands on that bloody Italian!" Syd would chase him with a rake, or a hoe, anything he could get his hands on, really.'

Bernard Morgans, who joined the groundstaff at the same time as Chinaglia, recalls one afternoon when Chinaglia 'borrowed' Tucker's mini-tractor while the groundsman was at lunch. 'He was driving it around the pitch and ended up putting it onto the concrete steps of one of the terraces and the tractor was written off. The wall between the pitch and terrace was only five or six inches high. There was murder over that but the club didn't find out who did it. We all covered for him.'

As an apprentice Chinaglia had a reputation for being a prankster. 'He used to move clothes around in the dressing-room,' adds Morgans, whose older brother, Ken, a Busby Babe who survived the Munich air crash, was one of Swansea's senior players. 'The first-team players would change out of their suits and when they had left the dressing-room, Giorgio would swap things around. The senior players didn't like that. He also used to hide Syd's barrow, stupid things like that.'

Webster, a striker signed from Manchester United in 1958 – he avoided the Munich tragedy earlier that year because he was at home bedridden with flu – noticed the groundstaff boy had already adopted bad habits. 'Some of the senior players and myself used to go for a drink in the town. All of a sudden Giorgio would walk into the same pub. I'd say to him, "Giorgio, you can't drink in here with us." He'd say, "Well, you do." And I'd tell him, "Yes, but we're has-beens! You're just starting. You mustn't let anyone see you having a pint." In those days people used to write to the manager saying they had seen players drinking. When I was in Manchester, if we wanted a drink we used to go out to Knutsford so we wouldn't be recognised. But Giorgio wouldn't listen. "If it's good enough for you, it's good enough for me," he said. Once he had something in his head you couldn't talk to him.'

David Ward, who regularly captained Swansea's Welsh League side, remembers another of Chinaglia's exploits. 'There used to be this cigarette machine in the "double-decker" stand. Along with some of the other lads, he would help himself to five Woodbines, using wire to get into the machine and pull out the cigarettes. There wasn't the stigma there is today about smoking and this machine was a sort of free supply for them. I think Giorgio was quite happy to go along with those kind of pranks. There was nothing malicious about it. It was just young lads with plenty of energy.'

Paul Crocker vividly remembers him filling up a condom with water and bouncing it around the wooden floor of the changing-room in front of the other apprentices.

Chinaglia started playing in the youth team, the Swansea Colts, but soon won a place in the Swansea Town 'A' side, a mixture of apprentices and trial players. The team was managed by John Irvine, a quantity surveyor from Cardiff. He was a former goalkeeper for Cardiff Corries, a well-known local league side in that city, and he was hugely popular among the 'A' side players. 'John had an eye for good players,' says Gordon Daniels. 'It was John who first recommended Chinaglia to us. He brought a number of Cardiff lads down to the Vetch – Mike Hayes, Mal Gilligan, Giorgio. They were very good players. Giorgio was just another schoolboy we brought in who was potentially a good player. We didn't know how famous he was going to become. If we did, perhaps we would have taken a lot more notice of him.'

Irvine's 'A' team played in the rough and ready Swansea Senior League which was made up of amateur teams from Swansea and the surrounding area, including Port Tennant Colts, Morriston Town, Merton Rovers, Mumbles Rangers, Swansea Boys' Club and Dilwyn Athletic. 'There's one thing that sticks in my mind about Giorgio,' recalls Billy O'Donald, outside-left in the 'A' team. 'He used to play on the right wing but for this one game at Skewen, our centre-forward, a lad from the Rhondda, didn't turn up so they put Giorgio there. That was his first game for the 'A' side and he scored six goals. That's where it all started for him.'

These local sides had their fair share of hatchetmen, as the young

Italian soon found out. 'In this league, and the Welsh League as well, all they wanted to do was kick you,' says Brian Thomas. 'In the 'A' team it was 17 year olds against grown men fresh out of the Army. They were fit, they were disciplined and there was no way they were going to let a kid called Giorgio Chinaglia take the piss out of them. To have an Italian playing in the Swansea Senior League was a novelty. It was like Pelé playing.'

For the amateur teams, the match against Swansea Town was the highlight of the season, a chance to put one over the professionals, 'the flippin' Swansea Town lot'. Adds Thomas, 'Giorgio was someone to be attacked. He could tumble around, mind. He could fall down like a good 'un whereas the local lads wouldn't fall down. Giorgio was playing continental football back then, he was 20 years ahead of his time. They couldn't handle that in Swansea. He was a good finisher and very skilful for his size but he was more suited to Italian football than British football. It would have been easier for him in the first team where he would be in the company of professionals. They let you have time on the ball and play football but in the Swansea Senior League all they wanted to do was kick you.'

Barrie Jones, who became the most expensive winger in British football in September 1964 when Plymouth Argyle agreed to pay Swansea Town £45,000 for his services, remembers watching the young Chinaglia in a midweek match. He was unimpressed. 'I saw him play once, on a Thursday afternoon,' explains Jones, who played 15 times for Wales. 'Some of the pros came with me to watch. The youth team was made up of groundstaff boys – maybe five or six – and the rest were lads who had a trade and came back to play some football. Giorgio looked a bit gangly and awkward to me. Easy to criticise but he didn't look anything special. He didn't contribute to the game. He didn't have any ball control and his first touch was really bad. He just slouched about with his head bowed.'

The next day Jones and full-back Harry Griffiths, a long-serving member of the first team, bumped into Chinaglia at the ground. 'I asked him what he thought of the game. He said he thought he had played fantastically. "I did this, I did that," he said. I turned to Harry and remarked that I must have been watching another game because, as far as I was concerned, Giorgio had looked very, very ordinary. If you were in the stand that day you would've looked at Giorgio and thought, "That kid has got no chance." Looking at players when they're 15 or 16, you can always tell if someone has got a little more than the average person and he didn't seem to have it.'

Jones may have caught Chinaglia on an off-day since the forward was beginning to make a name for himself in the Swansea Senior League. 'He was an out-and-out goalscorer,' says Colin Park. 'Give him the ball and wherever the net was he'd find it. He would score six and seven at a time. In one game we reached double figures and he scored seven. If he had three chances he'd put one of them away.'

Geoff Thomas adds, 'He became a bit of a name in this league and all the players would be trying to kick him. He wouldn't be having much of a game then all of a sudden – bang, bang – he'd score two goals. He wasn't a physical player. If the ball was flying into the box he wasn't the type to go diving in. But he had two good feet and loads of skill. A lot of Italians used to come and watch us because of Giorgio and they all loved him. I played loads of times with him and I thought to myself, "This boy's gonna make it!" I mean, he was the type who wouldn't have a kick all game, then he'd volley a goal from nowhere. He did have a knack of scoring goals.'

Tommy Jackson's abiding memory of the forward is a Welsh League game at Haverfordwest, a town in West Wales, when he turned their left-back Ray Davies inside out. 'Giorgio was playing wide on the right and he absolutely murdered him. Ray couldn't catch Giorgio, he'd be gone. Not only was he quick but he was clever too.'

The club appeared to have unearthed an exotic gem, swiped from under the noses of Cardiff City. Paul Crocker remarks, 'Giorgio was pretty successful because most of the under-18s played in the youth team but he regularly played in the 'A' side. They were basically playing against park players and winning by 10, 12 and even 15 goals and Giorgio was doing quite well.' Chinaglia played up front with the blond, burly John

Roberts who would later play in defence for Arsenal. Roberts was a typical British centre-forward – brave, bustling and willing to take knocks.

Chinaglia, on the other hand, boasted flashy skills and a penchant for scoring spectacular goals. 'He was one of the lads who was always trying to do tricks,' recalls Les Harris, a left-back at the club. 'We used to hit the ball up front to him and he'd try and flick it on or do an overhead kick, those sort of things.'

During the 1963–64 season, his second year at the club, Chinaglia broke into the Welsh League team. His goalscoring exploits for the 'A' team were finally rewarded. The opponents on his début were Bridgend, who were duly thumped 10–1. Chinaglia, who, according to the *South Wales Evening Post* match report, 'fitted in well with his more experienced colleagues', was involved in five of the goals, scoring twice and setting up three. 'You could see he had talent. It was just a case of nurturing it,' says Tommy Jackson. 'His ability was typically foreign. We'd rave about him now. To us he stood out. We knew he had ability but the management didn't and they let him go, which was unbelievable. If he had been anywhere else he would have been a big star straight away.'

His prowess in front of goal had caught the attention of the local press. Bill Paton, sports editor and football correspondent at the Swansea-based *Evening Post*, dubbed him 'the young Italian with the goalscoring touch'. Paton was not his only admirer. Pat Searle, the pipe-smoking football writer on the Welsh national newspaper, the *Western Mail* in Cardiff, took a keen interest in Chinaglia. A week after the Bridgend massacre, Searle wrote a glowing account of Chinaglia in his regular column, *The Swansea Scene*. 'One of the brightest stars on Swansea Town's books is Giorgio Chinaglia (pronounced Kin-al-ya) who could well develop into another John Charles. Son of a Cardiff chef, Giorgio is Italian born and bred, is over six foot, weighs 11 stone and possesses natural talent. Two weeks ago Mr Alan Hardaker, secretary of the Football League, inquired about Chinaglia. He wanted to know whether the boy was naturalised. Giorgio is still Italian and will play for Italy if he makes the grade.'

Searle continued, 'He needed a season to settle down. He looked good in patches, but now he has arrived. In his last five outings Giorgio has scored 13 goals. He got a couple in a Welsh League game last week.' According to the veteran hack, the teenage immigrant was being monitored by the Italian Football Association. 'In a letter to their representative in London, the Italians have asked for a report on Giorgio. He phoned me and I was able to tell him, "Chinaglia has the makings of a top-class player. He has a nice personality, a sporting instinct and is proud to be Italian – and Welsh!"'

John Harries remembers Searle's infatuation with Swansea's rising star. "Giorgio was well in with him, well in. He had some bloody good write-ups and they were things Giorgio never did. He would write, 'Giorgio Chinaglia scored a 35-yard goal". Giorgio couldn't kick the ball 35 yards! What happened was someone else fired a shot, the goalie would save it and Giorgio would just tap in the rebound. But in the paper it said he scored from 35 yards. We'd say, "What game was that then?" He had a good ally in Pat Searle.'

Despite the rave reports that season, Chinaglia progressed no further than the Welsh League. 'I see no reason why Chinaglia shouldn't make his first-team debut this season if he continues to improve,' said Trevor Morris in the autumn of 1963. Obviously, the striker did not do enough to convince the manager. 'Of course I should have played in the first team,' said Chinaglia years after he left the Vetch. 'But if you were 16 or 17, you couldn't play in the first team. Different era, different mentality. A lot of fans used to watch our reserve matches. A lot of Italians used to come and see me. We used to win 3–0, 4–0, 5–0. I used to score all the time but they never picked me in the first team. When the reserve games finished and we walked off the pitch, the opposition players used to joke with me, "Why aren't you in the first team?"'

In the league that season Chinaglia missed out on very little. The Swans had a dismal time, finishing 19th in the 22-team division, avoiding relegation by just one point. But he did miss out on a remarkable FA Cup campaign. This was the season Swansea reached the semi-finals and a place at Wembley was denied only by a fluke 40-yard goal scored by Preston's Tony Singleton, on a quagmire of a pitch at Villa Park in Birmingham.

The cup run started in January 1964, when Division Four side Barrow were easily beaten 4–1 at the Vetch. Then the Swans overcame two First Division teams, Sheffield United and Stoke City but the highlight came in the sixth round when they beat Bill Shankly's Liverpool at Anfield. The 'Morris Minors' silenced the Kop with a stunning 2–1 victory. The semi-final at Villa Park saw Swansea paired with fellow Second Division side Preston North End. Even though Preston were third and Swansea seventeenth, many tipped a Swansea victory. In the league the Welsh side hammered Preston 5–1 at the Vetch and drew 3–3 at Deepdale. 'All the reserves went on a special coach to Villa Park,' recalls Colin Park. 'On that day we didn't have a game so we all went up to watch the semi-final, including Giorgio. We had a police escort through the ground. I remember the club had all the tracksuits ready for the final. They were all white.'

It had rained continually in Birmingham the week of the semi-final and the Villa Park pitch was a mudbath. Nevertheless, Jimmy McLaughlin sent the 30,000 Swansea supporters into ecstasy when he fired his team ahead a minute before half-time. But after the interval the tide turned. Alex Dawson equalised from the penalty spot before Tony Singleton, Preston's red-haired centre-half, hit a speculative shot which caught goalkeeper Noel Dwyer, a hero at Anfield, off his line. 'Before the match we arranged to meet up with the first-team players and their wives after the game,' adds Park. 'But we lost so we came back on our own. We stopped somewhere and had a drink ourselves. We were very despondent. It was a very sad day.'

CHAPTER FOUR

AFTER TWO YEARS of sweeping stands and being buffeted and bashed in Swansea Senior League matches, Chinaglia had his sights set on winning a first-team place during the 1964–65 season. It would not be easy. Swansea Town had 36 players on its books and Morris was not one for tinkering with the team. 'You had to wait and wait to get into the first team,' explains Mike Hayes. 'Today they throw them in at 16 or 17, but then you weren't given a chance until you were 18 or 19.'

There was an air of inevitability about Morris's selections and, frustratingly for Chinaglia, he rarely deviated from a forward line that consisted of Jimmy McLaughlin, Eddie Thomas, Keith Todd, Derek Draper and Brian Evans. 'Trevor Morris, I felt, was a first-team man. If you weren't in the first-team he was very difficult to get hold of,' continues Hayes. 'In one public trial match – first team against the second team – it ended 0–0 and a few of the second-team lads had a really good game. But there was no way we were going to get into that first team. Morris was set in his ways. Every morning he would walk around the training ground with the captain, Mike Johnson. I think they picked the team between them. It used to happen in those days, the captain had a lot to do with who was in and who was out. I had to wait a year to get into the first team and it was the same for Giorgio. They wouldn't take too many chances with the youngsters. At the end of a season, in the last couple of games, you might get a run-out if the team was safe.'

The first-team players, most of whom had families to feed and mortgages to pay, had much to lose if they were dethroned. They would instantly lose the £5 appearance fee and an additional £4 bonus for a win or £2 for a draw. 'If you played in the first team,' explains Keith Todd, one of the first-team forwards, 'and you won, then you basically doubled your money. And if you played a midweek game and won that as well, then it was treble wages. This is what we played for.'

Players established in the first team fought to keep their position. Alan Wilkins recalls one practice match. 'Mal Gilligan went past Harry Griffiths on the left wing and I heard Harry say to "Gilli", "If you go past me again you're fuckin' dead." Harry was a first-team player and one of the Welsh League players was taking him to the cleaners. Harry had three kids and if he was out of the first team his money would have dropped drastically.'

Since the Italian was a direct threat to his place, Todd took a keen interest in Chinaglia's progress. He first noticed him in a public trial match which took place pre-season. 'I thought to myself, "Good God, I'm gonna have to play for my place!" He was absolutely brilliant. His ball control was unbelievable. He had a lot more talent than me and I'm not ashamed to say that. He was bigger than me, he was faster than me and his ball control was amazing, especially for someone so young. He was the best young player I ever saw at the Vetch.'

During the summer Chinaglia had moved to Swansea and was in digs with Alan Wilkins, in a terraced house in Cromwell Street, not far from the Vetch. There were several reasons why he had stopped commuting from Cardiff. First, his scooter partner, Paul Crocker, who had fitness problems and who sensed he was making no progress in the game, quit football to pursue a career in engineering. Second, Morris preferred his players to live near the ground. Third, he would be away from the watchful eyes of his parents, especially his strict father. It was the Swinging '60s and Chinaglia was a tall, young and handsome football player. 'All the girls round here were after him,' says

Dolly Phillips. 'There used to be a gang of girls hanging around the front gates all the time. They used to wait outside for the players, especially Giorgio.' Her terraced house adjacent to the ground was the perfect vantage point: 'I used to call him Casanova because he was one for the women.'

Chinaglia's stay in Cromwell Street did not last long, as Wilkins explains. 'We'd done our pre-season training and we were on our way home. Giorgio had his grumpy head on because he hadn't been picked for a practice match. He was very temperamental and he was kicking things on the pavement, throwing stones and cursing to himself. Our landlady always made us salad for lunch and sure enough, as we walked in, there was salad on the table. Giorgio saw it, hit the table and shouted, "Not fuckin' salad again!" He didn't know the landlady was right behind him, walking out of the kitchen. She hadn't gone in to work that day. She kicked him out of the digs but said I could stay. "You can stay, Alan – but he'll have to go!" He seemed to throw tantrums more than anybody else. He'd chuck things about and lose his temper.'

Wilkins remained loyal to Chinaglia and they searched for new accommodation, eventually moving in with Mike Hayes and Mal Gilligan in Rhondda Street, which was the next street up from Cromwell Street. The house was owned by a 65-year-old woman who lived there with her elderly mother. 'When we asked to move in I remember the landlady saying, "Oh, but I can't do any Italian cooking!" I told her Giorgio wouldn't mind.'

Chinaglia shared the top floor with the landlady's mother, in a bedroom next door to hers. 'Giorgio was scared stiff of the old lady. She was well into her eighties, maybe even nineties, and she used to freak Giorgio out. Mal Gilligan used to pretend he was the old woman and he'd knock on his door, put on an old lady's voice and say, "Sonny, sonny." Giorgio used to go mad. We used to wind him up as well, saying she used to go walking in the night and if he saw her wandering about to help her back to her room.' Chinaglia's response to their teasing was to say, 'I can't handle her. She does my head in.'

Gilligan remembers the young forward becoming friendly with a married woman who lived nearby. 'This woman was about 32 and Giorgio was only 17. Her husband used to go out playing golf and he'd pop over the road. He got chatty with her. We used to have every afternoon off and we'd go and play snooker at a club down the road, but Giorgio was always over there talking to her. I think he was knocking her off, or trying to knock her off. There was every reason to think that.' Hayes sheds further light on the relationship: 'He fancied her. When the husband was gone he was over there, carrying on, I presume. I know he was there all the time. When he came back to the house he always had a smile on his face.'

Chinaglia began the season flitting once more between the 'A' team and the Welsh League side. The first team had fallen into the relegation zone after collecting just three points from the first seven games, but instead of trying some of the reserve players Morris delved into the transfer market. October 1965 brought some depressing news for Chinaglia. Morris had paid £13,000 to Coventry City for a big, bustling striker called George Kirby. Chinaglia's eye had been on the centre-forward's jersey since August, when Eddie Thomas was sold to Derby County. Now Kirby was in his way.

'If they didn't think you were good enough they bought somebody and once they did that they had to play them. They were in,' explains Brian Thomas. 'In my case they bought Albert Harley for £15,000 from Shrewsbury Town and that was the end for me. I couldn't get back in. They bought Kirby and he would have been a block for Giorgio. If you bought someone in those days he had to play in the first team otherwise people would have a go at you for buying a player and then not using him. I imagine Kirby was a nail in Giorgio's coffin. He was also a forward who dived here and there whereas Giorgio wasn't like that.'

As far as Chinaglia was concerned, Kirby epitomised British football's preference for a physical style. 'He was strong in the air and good with the elbows,' says Chinaglia. 'He was useless with his feet but he would get stuck in. But we want football, not wrestling matches.'

Chinaglia demonstrated the ability to become a professional player but there were question marks over his dedication. He was certainly a poor trainer and this may have been a reason for Morris's reluctance to throw him into the league side. 'Giorgio was never really – how can I say? – in love with it,' says Mike Hayes. 'He went through the motions. Whether he thought he was going to go somewhere else I don't know. I never found him full of enthusiasm for Swansea. I don't think he cared, to be honest. I'm sure he would've loved to have played in the first team but my initial impression was that he didn't care.'

His former Swansea team-mates all agree that Chinaglia, despite the odd flashes of brilliance, was lazy in training and during matches. 'He was a nice guy,' says David Ward, 'but he was laid-back and everything was just a little too much trouble. Giorgio was a bit of an enigma. He had everything going for him – he had the build, the physique, the ball control – but his attitude was not what it should have been. He was round-shouldered and he waddled and slouched about. I'm sure this bloody round-shouldered appearance was because of his general attitude to life.

'I played with Giorgio on a number of occasions and he was one you had to keep shouting and screaming at throughout the game,' continues Ward. 'You had to tell him to pull his finger out and chase back. He'd just go and hide. He wanted to be on the end of crosses, he wanted the glory but he didn't want to do any of the work. When he wanted he could play, but most of the time he appeared in the game infrequently. You'd lose him for a long time and you'd end up calling him things you probably wouldn't get away with today – you Italian this, you Italian that.'

The forward was beginning to lose interest at Swansea, disenchanted with the style of football being played and being passed over for the Football League side. 'He'd get a rollicking at half-time but it seemed to be water off a duck's back,' says Ward. 'It never seemed to make any impression. When he got a rollicking he'd wave his hands about, shrug his shoulders and shout a bit of Italian. He'd gee up for five or ten minutes, then go back to his old ways.' Ward recalls a Welsh League game against Haverfordwest. 'Giorgio wanted to take everything, every free-kick, every corner. He wanted to try and bend it round the wall or chip it, but nothing was coming off. If only you could get through to Giorgio that he should play as part of a side he would have looked so much better.'

Roy Saunders, a former Liverpool half-back who played with Chinaglia in several Welsh League matches, says, 'He had so much ability and skill but he was too carefree. He'd have a good chance of scoring but instead of just hitting the ball he'd flick it up in the air and try an overhead kick.' (The career of Saunders' son, Dean, was to mirror that of Chinaglia. A speedy striker, he was given a free transfer from the Vetch in 1985 but, like the Italian two decades before him, he would find fame and fortune elsewhere.) 'For a manager running a football team Giorgio was a real headache,' continues Saunders. 'He'd do daft things. Instead of just tapping it into the net he'd backheel it, or try a scissors-kick. He had to do something clever and that didn't go down too well. They wanted effort. The coaches were on at him every day but he wouldn't listen. It was like talking to a brick wall. There's nothing worse than seeing someone unmarked and, instead of passing to him, flicking the ball up and trying a shot. He was a very selfish player. When he had the ball he didn't want anyone else to have it. He wasn't a team player. He also wanted everything laid on a plate for him. He wouldn't run after the ball. He expected the other players, the donkeys, to do the grafting.'

Chinaglia gained a reputation as one of the worst trainers at the club. As the squad lapped the Skewen dog track, the tall, lumbering Italian was always at the back. He showed no enthusiasm for sprint work and took short-cuts during cross-country runs to the Mumbles, a picturesque seaside suburb of Swansea and popular tourist destination. 'He was really lazy in training. He wouldn't knuckle down. That was one of his problems,' says Saunders. 'We used to run to the Mumbles and back, along Mumbles Road.' The players would turn around at The Apple – an outdoor novelty snack bar shaped like an apple, near Mumbles Pier. Anyone who took more than an hour to complete the run would be made to jog 12 laps around the Vetch. 'I later found out Giorgio was getting lifts back on a milk float or any vehicle which was passing at the time. He probably wouldn't have done the run in an hour and he wanted to get out of doing the 12 laps.'

Mike Hayes, who was part of Chinaglia's running group, adds, 'On some of the runs we'd take a bottle of pop, milk and chocolate biscuits because it was so boring. We'd stop half-way, sit and wait. Then we'd join the front-runners on their way back.'

Another jogging route was along Mumbles Road and up a steep hill which led to Singleton Hospital, which overlooks the sweeping Swansea Bay. 'We had to go up and around the hospital,' recalls Colin Park, 'but Giorgio wouldn't go all the way up. He'd cut across the park below the hospital. We also had to cross a pedestrian bridge – up one set of steps, over and down the next set of steps. He missed a few of those. He was a poor trainer, Giorgio. He was one of the worst at the club, along with Noel Dwyer.'

The Italian's apathy regarding training had not gone unnoticed. One morning, Roy Saunders tried an experiment to make him work harder. 'We used to sprint to one corner flag, then we'd jog to the other. Then we'd sprint, then jog again,' he explains. 'Giorgio used to start at the front and drop back until, at the end, he'd be right at the very back. So to try and stop him dropping back I deliberately ran behind him. When he tried to drop back I pushed him forward. I did this for three or four laps. Then I pushed him again and he turned round. I could see in his face that if I touched him again he was going to fill me in. "Hang on, I'd better watch it here!" I said to myself. He was a big lad so I left him alone.'

Chinaglia was not an early riser. Walter Robbins described him as a 'heavy sleeper' and his poor punctuality infuriated Trevor Morris and his successor, Glyn Davies. 'He had trouble getting up in the morning and that didn't go down too well,' says Tommy Jackson. 'That was half the reason he didn't get on at the Vetch. Sometimes he didn't surface until lunchtime. He just couldn't get up. Getting out of bed didn't agree with him. The club would send people up to his digs. They'd knock on his window but there would be no movement. He wouldn't roll in late every day, just certain days.' His all-night card sessions were mostly to blame for his lethargy in the mornings. Chinaglia played poker with his Italian friends at a house in Carlton Terrace. 'We'd play until three, four, even five in the morning,' recalls Mario Maccarinelli, who befriended Chinaglia while he was living in Swansea. 'We used to meet in the Continental Café at 7.30 p.m. or 8 p.m. and then go to this house – me, Giorgio, two other Italians and this Welsh boy. We used to put four or five pounds on the table and then gamble a shilling at a time.'

Maccarinelli used to ask the modestly-paid apprentice where his money came from. 'My mother gave me money without my father knowing and my father gave me money without my mother knowing,' was the response. 'I used to ask him, "Why are you staying up all night when you have to train in the morning?" And he would say, "Don't worry about it, I play good. I always play good." He was a hell of a boy! He was always bored. His mum and dad were in Cardiff and he was living in digs. I don't think he wanted to go home.'

Chinaglia spent most of his free time with Alan Wilkins. They resembled a comedy double-act – Chinaglia was tall, lean and dark while Wilkins was short, stocky and fair. 'Giorgio wasn't the type of lad to go to the local clubs and have a beer. A new nightclub was more up his street,' says Wilkins. 'We used to play a lot of snooker. We'd pay for the lights. He always wanted a two-black start because he said I was better than him. Sometimes we'd go to the Electricity Club, put two beer crates down and have a game, just me and him. Giorgio was very conscious of his appearance. He loved his clothes. He'd buy a pink shirt whereas people in Swansea wouldn't wear pink. He'd buy all the modern stuff. I remember he bought a trilby once. The lads used to take the mick out of him and call him "The Italian Wonder".'

Chinaglia and Wilkins were the most mischievous members of Swansea's squad and often found themselves summoned to Morris's office, deep inside the bowels of the Vetch. 'Giorgio had a Lambretta and it was club policy not to ride a motorbike or scooter,' recalls Wilkins. 'One day I twisted my ankle on the kerb while getting off Giorgio's scooter. It blew up like a balloon. When Trevor found out about my ankle he called me in. "You're playing for other teams on a Sunday or midweek, aren't you?" In fact, we were. This guy living opposite us ran a football team and they had this big cup game coming up. He asked me and Giorgio if we would play. "Nobody will know," he said. We did play, just to get a game. But I didn't get the injury playing in that game, it was genuinely from getting off the Lambretta. "Honestly, boss, I did it on Giorgio's scooter." Trevor said, "That scooter had better go back to your digs and stay there!" So Giorgio had to put it away and stop riding it.'

The duo also incurred the wrath of Steve Leavy, who was the biggest disciplinarian on Morris's coaching staff. On Thursday and Friday nights, when players were ordered to rest at home for Saturday's matches, the Irishman would drive down to the Mumbles and search the Embassy and Pier Ballrooms to see if the curfew had been broken. 'Giorgio and I went to the pictures on a Friday night. We were playing in a Welsh League game the next day,' explains Wilkins. 'As we came out Giorgio wanted a bottle of pop to take home. We went to a pub, the Builders Arms, and there was a load of Italians in there playing cards. They were playing three-card brag and chucking all this money in. We stayed in there for about 10 minutes to see who won the kitty. The next morning at the ground Steve pointed at each of us and said, "You're not playing and you're not playing." He told us, "You were in the Builders last night drinking." I said, "On my mother's life, we just bought a bottle of pop." He replied, "OK, I'll look at your performances. If they're no good I'll know you were drinking." Thankfully we did all right.'

On 14 October, a cold Wednesday night in South Yorkshire, Chinaglia was finally selected to play in the first team. He played outside-right in a League Cup match against Rotherham at Millmoor. Rotherham were a decent Second Division side and would finish the season in seventh place, but it was no surprise to see Morris throw Chinaglia in for this long, unappealing midweek trip north. At the time the League Cup, launched in 1960 and the brainchild of Alan Hardaker, the Football League secretary, was treated with derision.

Dubbed 'Hardaker's Horror' because it added to an already congested programme, five of the country's top clubs – Arsenal, Sheffield Wednesday, Tottenham Hotspur, Wolves and West Bromwich Albion – refused to take part.

It was an ideal match for Morris to test some of his youngsters and John Roberts was another player given his first-team début, at centre-forward. The Swans drew 2–2 and Chinaglia gave a reasonable performance. In a bad-tempered game which saw six players booked, the Italian provided Swansea's equaliser three minutes from time, his 'well-flighted corner' finding the head of centre-half Mike Johnson. Despite what Pat Searle described in the *Western Mail* as 'an encouraging performance', he had to wait four months for his next taste of first-team action. Herbie Williams, a left-half who made more than 500 appearances for the Swans, remembers Chinaglia's début. 'It was a very difficult match for him. Rotherham was a tough place to go. Giorgio was always knocking on Trevor's door asking him when he was going to play. After this game Trevor said to him, "Are you still going to come knocking on my door now?" which I thought was a little bit harsh.'

Not long after his son signed for Swansea, Mario Chinaglia had left the hotel trade to open his own restaurant. Located on the edge of the city centre, it was called Mario's Bamboo Room. The chairs were bamboo, there were bamboo canes along the walls and even the picture frames were made from the tropical stem. Mario Chinaglia was the owner and the chef. His wife helped in the kitchen and he employed two waiters, one Spanish and the other Austrian. He served basic but popular food of the time – minestrone soup, prawn cocktail (in a glass goblet), paté on toast, risotto, veal with spaghetti Bolognese, steak Diane, steak chasseur and T-bone steak.

It quickly became one of the busiest establishments in the city (mainly because it stayed open so late rather than for the quality of its food) and was especially popular with local footballers. One of its regular customers was John Charles, the former Juventus forward who was now playing for Cardiff City.

The restaurant, a favourite among the Italian, Jewish and Maltese communities (it remained open until 1977, the year the Chinaglia family moved to the United States to live with Giorgio, when he was playing for New York Cosmos), had a curious design. A flight of stairs led customers from the front door to a landing which comprised the kitchen and several tables. There were two rooms on either side of the kitchen. The regulars used the room on the right while infrequent customers were seated in the room on the left, which was reached by a second flight of stairs. Although he held only a normal licence which allowed him to trade until 11 p.m., Mario Chinaglia would stay open to 'members', his friends and regulars, allowing them to carry on eating, drinking and playing cards until 4 or 5 a.m. After 11 p.m. Andrea Delnero, who had left the steelworks to work in the Bamboo Room as Chinaglia's right-hand man, kept his eye on the front door from the landing. When the bell rang he would look through the glass partition and any 'member' would be granted access.

In February 1965, Chinaglia's father made the first of a series of trips to the Vetch Field in his dark-green Rover. His son had turned 18 and Mario was unhappy he was not a first-team regular. Since the previous summer, he had let it be known that he wanted Swansea to release him so he could play for an Italian club. Mario Chinaglia claimed several Italian clubs were interested in signing Giorgio. 'I don't think he has progressed fast enough with Swansea Town and as there is a good job waiting for him in Italy,' he said in a newspaper interview. 'I hope Mr Morris will see my point of view.'

Chinaglia scored 50 goals during 1963–64 and during the summer holidays in Carrara he was a guest player in a football youth tournament. According to Chinaglia senior, his son caught the attention of three *Serie A* clubs – Juventus, Torino and reigning champions Bologna – as well as two *Serie B* clubs, Modena and Reggiana. 'I see no reason why Giorgio shouldn't be released,' he told reporters. 'He is an Italian by nationality and his heart is with that country. I don't think Swansea Town will stand in his way.'

But the club did stand in his way. After nurturing the player for two years, it was not about to release him. 'There were rules and regulations governing junior players,' recalls Trevor Morris, 'but his father wanted this and he wanted that. The way his father talked, and the things he wanted, you would have thought Giorgio was an Italian international. His dad was a great big chap. Typical Italian. I always knew when he entered my office because it suddenly went dark. We had some heated chats but it never came to blows, although I was told that he was going to come down with his meat cleaver and use it on me.' (On a separate occasion John Hedges remembers Chinaglia's father arriving at the ground carrying his meat cleaver and looking for the club secretary, Gordon Daniels. 'For some reason Giorgio wasn't given the win bonus so his father came down with this massive machete,' says Hedges. 'He asked me where Gordon was and said, "Why Giorgio not have the bonus?" I said I didn't know where Gordon was. He asked a few other people where he was but no one knew. He stayed at the ground quite a long time, then he left because he couldn't find Gordon.')

Discussions concerning a professional contract for Giorgio provided Mario Chinaglia with another chance to wrestle his son away from the struggling Second Division club. Morris offered the striker £20 a week, the standard rate for newly qualified professionals. 'I believe the terms we offered were quite adequate for an 18 year old,' remarked Morris at the time. This did not go down too well in the Bamboo Room. 'The terms they have suggested to my boy are not good enough, and unless they agree to increase the offer then he will finish at the Vetch Field and go back to Italy where there are a number of clubs who want him,' warned his father. 'I've just returned from Italy and know there are at least six clubs in the second and third divisions who would sign him up.'

Chinaglia himself wanted to stay with the Swans. In the *Western Mail* he told Pat Searle, 'It's all very distressing. I want to stay with Swansea Town but my father seems to have other ideas.' The *Evening Post* seemed convinced he would be leaving. 'FAREWELL GOALS FOR CHINAGLIA' said the headline after he scored twice in Swansea's 4–2 win at Haverfordwest in a Welsh league match in early March. Everybody thought it was his last game for the Welsh club.

The dispute went as far as the Football League's offices in London, and nearly two months later, in April, Alan Hardaker ruled in favour of the club. If Chinaglia left the Vetch he could not join another professional club for two years. Defeated, Mario Chinaglia had to watch his son sign professional forms with Swansea Town. The alternative was to watch him spend 24 months in the wilderness. Football League rules stipulated that a player was forbidden from joining another professional club until two years after completion of his apprenticeship.

Looking back, Morris says, 'It's only natural for a father to think so well of his children but he wanted a lot more than we were entitled to give him. Giorgio was only an up-and-coming youngster but his dad thought he was the greatest player in the world – a genius.' Although Morris recognised the striker's ability he was also aware of his flaws. 'He never helped out his colleagues. He never went looking for the ball, it had to come to him. He was overgrown and to look at him you'd think he couldn't do anything, but he was very good on the ball. He could go past his man, which you couldn't get many players to do.'

At the height of the row between father and club, Chinaglia made his league début against Portsmouth at the Vetch in February 1965. Keith Todd injured his shoulder in a Welsh Cup game against Pwllheli and Chinaglia had staked his claim the previous week, scoring four goals in the 7–1 win over Pembroke Borough in the Welsh League. Despite the ill feeling between Mario Chinaglia and Trevor Morris, the manager invited Giorgio's father to the game as a special guest. Chinaglia senior declined, saying he was 'too busy', but before he put the phone down he told Morris he would be coming to Swansea the following week 'to discuss his son's contract'.

A win was vital for both teams. 'Pompey' were bottom while Swansea were one place above them. The teams were level on points although Portsmouth had played one more game than Morris's side. For the Swans, and Chinaglia personally, it proved to be a frustrating afternoon. In front of 9,000 people – a bus strike was blamed for the below-average attendance – the visitors ground out a 0–0 draw. Marking Chinaglia that day was Portsmouth's veteran captain, Jimmy

Dickinson. A former England international, the 39-year-old defender had more than 800 league games under his belt. As Pat Searle reminded his readers, 'Dickinson was playing football before Giorgio Chinaglia was born.' He had no intention of being fooled by a teenager who had just served his apprenticeship.

The Italian started the match at centre-forward but after an ineffective first-half was moved to inside-right. 'Chinaglia was finding the occasion a little too much for him,' wrote Bill Paton in the *Evening Post*, 'which was hardly surprising for he was facing one of the most experienced players in the game, and a first-class defender.' Swansea's Ken Pound, who was switching wings, fired some good crosses into the Portsmouth penalty box, all to no avail. 'Dickinson was the master in the middle,' said Paton, 'and Chinaglia was being given little scope'. He was replaced by Peter Davies. 'He [Chinaglia] never got a kick because they packed their defence,' said John Irvine, when asked about Chinaglia's league début in an interview in 1972.

Seven minutes from time, Davies won a penalty after he was obstructed inside the box. Jimmy McLaughlin's weak shot was easily saved by John Milkins and 'Pompey' drove back to the south coast with a precious point. 'It was the same old story,' added Paton, 'of a tight defence proving too good for a forward line which showed little method.'

Chinaglia had failed to take his chance. His former team-mates believe the absence of superior Combination football, coupled with the out-of-date coaching methods, were to blame for his lacklustre performances. 'In the Combination we were playing First Division sides,' explains John Harries. 'The Welsh League was no competition really. Dropping out of the Combination was one of Trevor Morris's money-saving ideas. That was his downfall, I think. He put business before football. Money came first. He should have been a general manager and let someone else run the first team. Walter did most of the work, but make Walter a cup of tea and you could get away with murder. When I think about it, there wasn't much professionalism down there at the time. When I left school I was playing for the Welsh Schools but I came to the Vetch and my career went backwards.'

Morris's rationale for withdrawing from the Combination was simple – these matches cost just as much in travel and accommodation as first-team games but there was no incoming revenue and the club's overdraft was almost thirty thousand pounds. The decision may have reduced costs but there is no doubt it hampered the development of young players such as Chinaglia. Instead of going head-to-head with professionals they were forced to play part-timers at village grounds. 'You'd be playing teams like Gwynfy, Haverfordwest and Milford Haven,' recalls former goalkeeper John Black, who joined the Swans from Arsenal in 1964 and became a close friend of Chinaglia. 'These teams had players who were past their sell-by date. Giorgio wasn't a good player in the Welsh League because there were too many people hacking him to death. He was never going to look good. We'd turn up and they'd look at the programme and see Giorgio Chinaglia, a 17-year-old Italian who's supposed to be the best thing since sliced bread. The first thing they did was give him a dig. That was the end of Giorgio because you never got any protection from the referee in those days.'

Reserve player Les Harris agrees that dropping out of the Combination was bad news for the Welsh League players. Instead of facing Arsenal Reserves at Highbury or Tottenham Reserves at White Hart Lane, they were taken to football backwaters such as Ton Pentre and Ebbw Vale. 'There was a huge gulf between the Welsh League and the Second Division. We were annihilating everyone in the Welsh League,' says Harris. 'I remember beating Bridgend 8–0. I don't think we ever lost a game! The gulf was so immense, it was ridiculous. Everything at Swansea was very slapdash. We trained for a couple of hours in the morning and it wasn't very meaningful. We rarely used the ball, it was run around the field. Giorgio was very individualistic. I think he needed one-to-one coaching, which didn't exist at the time. He needed someone who would take him under his wing. If he was at a First Division club, such as Arsenal or Tottenham, I'm sure he wouldn't have gone back to Italy.'

The Portsmouth match was Chinaglia's final first-team appearance that season. The following week Todd returned to the side and

Chinaglia stepped back into the reserves. While playing for Swansea's Welsh League side he found himself facing some of his old Cardiff Schools team-mates. Richie Morgan, who was playing centre-half for Cardiff Corries before joining Cardiff City, was one of them. 'He was physically stronger but he was still the same Giorgio who had played for Cardiff Schools. In those days we were allowed to rule a little bit by intimidation and Giorgio was one of those players you could intimidate pretty easily if you got a tackle in early.'

Morgan remembers him constantly moaning to the referee and making demonstrative gestures whenever he was roughly challenged by a defender. 'Giorgio used to say, "Football is not meant to be like this. Football is an art." Or, "You British don't play the game properly" and "Don't kick me. If you do I'll kick you." He always wanted an extra touch – that encouraged you to kick him and we duly obliged. Give him a good kicking and you could go home because Giorgio would drift back to the half-way line. Somebody obviously got hold of him after he left Swansea and sorted him out.'

With just four league games remaining, Morris's side looked certain for relegation. But they won the first three which meant they could stay in Division Two if they beat mid-table Coventry City at Highfield Road and Swindon Town and Portsmouth both lost their games. In the event, results elsewhere did not matter. Swansea were beaten 3–0 and consigned to Third Division football for the first time since 1949. Inevitably, Morris paid the ultimate price. 'We think that after seven years a change of manager will benefit the club,' announced Swansea chairman Philip Holden. 'We have terminated Mr Morris's engagement and will now advertise the post.' Asked how he felt about Morris's dismissal, Chinaglia replies, 'I didn't care that much. I had to get on with my career. I didn't care who came or who went.'

The relegation prompted a clear-out. Chinaglia's name was one of the 20 on the retained list while seven players were given free transfers. They included Alan Wilkins and Mike Hayes. Chinaglia would have to continue at the Vetch without two of his best friends.

CHAPTER FIVE

THE MAN CHOSEN to replace Trevor Morris was Swansea-born Glyn Davies. Davies, a former Swansea player, was 33 years old when he was lured back home from non-league club Yeovil Town, where he had been player-manager for two years. He was moderately successful with the Southern League club, leading them to fourth place. 'We think we have chosen the right man,' enthused Trevor Wood, the club's vice-chairman, to the Press. Those words would haunt Wood for the rest of his days. In his first season Davies nearly took the Swans into the Fourth Division. He would also release Chinaglia, the forward whose goals would win Roman club Lazio their first-ever championship (and who would be valued at a record-breaking £800,000), on a free transfer.

A versatile footballer, Davies had played centre-half, wing-half and full-back and gained a reputation for being a ferocious tackler and tireless grafter. He spent his best playing days at the Baseball Ground with Derby County, winning the Division Three (North) championship in 1957 before joining the Swans five years later. During his one season at the Vetch, he was never considered a first-team regular and ended up playing his fair share of Welsh League games. Davies and Chinaglia already knew each other. Chinaglia was on the groundstaff when his new manager was a player.

'When Glyn was a player and Giorgio was a groundstaff boy, they really used to row,' remembers Gary Owen, who joined the groundstaff a year after Chinaglia. 'Glyn would go on about Italians and the Catholic thing, then Giorgio would rattle back something in Italian. They didn't like each other at all. Giorgio did have these battles with people. They'd take the mick out of him, going on about the Pope and Catholics. He'd storm off. He didn't like it one bit. Giorgio had a very strong Italian nature – very emotional and very highly strung.'

Owen recalls one argument between Davies and Chinaglia, in the changing-rooms at the Vetch. 'I remember this as if it was yesterday. The dressing-rooms were used by the players to change for training and you could walk through the home dressing-room, through the visitors' one, and out through a back door. One day I was walking through with some of the other apprentices and Giorgio was going out of this back door. He didn't close it after him and Glyn shouted out, "You dopey bastard, shut the door!" Giorgio came back and had a right go at Glyn. Giorgio took it personally. It was very unpleasant, a real shouting match. When Glyn came back as the manager everyone was winding Giorgio up, saying things like, "Hey, Giorgio, he doesn't like you" and "Now you're in trouble".'

Swansea was not the most cosmopolitan of towns and the Second World War, which had ended only 20 years earlier, had generated a degree of anti-Italian feeling. Chinaglia was sometimes taunted during games by spectators. Alan Wilkins remembers an incident in the town centre while they were travelling to their favourite snooker hall after finishing training. 'Giorgio was giving me a backie on his Lambretta and we were about to arrive at the snooker centre in Wind Street when all of a sudden he jumped off – the scooter was still moving – and he thumped this bloke. It was someone who had called him an "ice cream wally" during a game. Giorgio recognised him and clocked him.'

When Davies succeeded Morris, he became the club's first-ever Swansea-born manager. He was picked from more than fifty applicants, among whom were experienced managers such as Eric Houghton, whose Aston Villa team beat Manchester United's 'Busby

Babes' in the 1957 FA Cup final; Walter Galbraith, who had done excellent work at Accrington Stanley and Bradford Park Avenue; and Eddie Lowe, who was working as a purchasing manager for a central, heating firm after a bad spell as player-manager of Notts County. When asked if there would be problems managing men he had played with just over a year ago, Davies replied, 'I intend to make it quite clear to everyone that I am the manager.' His method, however, alienated the players. Alan Jones, an emerging centre-half at the Vetch, recalls, 'On his first day he got us all into the dressing-room and said, "I'm the boss. You either call me Mr Davies or boss. You don't call me Glyn." It didn't go down too well. From the very beginning he got off on the wrong footing.'

Davies brought with him Tommy Casey as his assistant, with Walter Robbins relegated to Welsh League and scouting duties. Casey, a wing-half from Belfast and the workhorse in Newcastle United's FA Cup-winning side of 1955, shared the same philosophy as Davies. He believed in hard training off the field, hard work on it. His maxim was, 'Be fit, have a healthy mind and body, and work hard all the time.' Casey and the laid-back Chinaglia would never see eye-to-eye.

'They asked me if I was interested in the job,' explains Davies. 'Initially I was, but there was a part of me that wasn't. They had just been relegated. I knew there were problems. I thought long and hard about it. My wife was from Swansea and she wanted to come back, but on reflection I should have stayed at Yeovil, for a little longer at least. I realised very quickly that things weren't going to turn out as I thought because of the situation in the boardroom. If you have a boardroom that's conducive to running a successful football team and prepared to finance the side correctly then you've got a chance. But the Swansea boardroom then wasn't strong. There was no money available. The chairman wasn't very well – he had Parkinson's Disease – and he relied on advice from other directors and one or two of them were not very football-minded. There was an overdraft limit and that limit had been reached before I got there. I didn't know these facts. You find these things out after you arrive. As with all clubs, you get promised things which don't materialise when you arrive. The FA Cup run in 1964 papered over the cracks. We needed three or four players in certain positions.'

In order to appease the disillusioned supporters – and help the lethargic season-ticket sales – Davies brought Ivor Allchurch back to Swansea, signing him from Cardiff City for £6,000. By now the classy inside-forward was 36 but he was the idol of the fans and, as his 15 goals in 27 games for Cardiff the previous season suggested, he was still more than useful.

But with no more money available, Davies either had to field the same players who took Swansea down or experiment with some of the youngsters. Inevitably, he took a close look at Chinaglia.

'He had a lot of promise, a lot of talent, which needed to be channelled in the right direction,' says Davies. 'I remember him as an apprentice with a lot of promise. My first impression of Giorgio was that he was someone who could be worked on and, everything being equal, made into a good player. But as I discovered, there were a lot of things not right in his make-up, not all of them his own doing. I knew his father was an unsettling influence on him.'

Davies was aware that there was a history between Chinaglia and the club. 'Trevor had problems with him. When he turned pro I don't think his father wanted him to sign. He wanted him to leave Swansea. He saw it as a stepping-stone club. He wanted him back in Italy and all this had been bubbling and boiling before I came.'

With Mike Hayes and Alan Wilkins shown the door, and Mal Gilligan having joined Bath City before the summer purge, Chinaglia started looking for new digs. He left the now lonely house in Rhondda Street to rent a bedsit in Glanmor Road, still in the Uplands area of the town. He now started to socialise with a different group of players – John Black, Geoff Thomas and Alan Jones. 'We always gambled,' admits Black. 'There would be Geoff, Giorgio and myself. We'd be skint by the end of the week and Thursday night was our night out. We usually went to the Park Hotel, where a local band would be playing. But by the Thursday we'd be broke, so we'd pool our money for a train fare back to Cardiff so Giorgio could go to his father's place and borrow some money. I think it was no more than a fiver, just so we could go out on the piss on a Thursday night. We used to bet a lot on horses because there were no dogs in those days. We weren't very clever and nine times out of ten we'd lose our money. Alan was shrewder than the rest of us. He wasn't a gambler.

'Everything was close together on High Street. We used to eat in the Continental Café, play snooker in the Castle Snooker Hall further up, then go into the betting shop a few doors down and then you had the railway station! The trip to Cardiff became a regular one for Giorgio but we'd pay him back the following week.'

Chinaglia's appetite for gambling was well known among his team-mates. Everything had to be for money – cards, snooker, horses. Gary Owen adds, 'He'd gamble on anything. He played snooker, loved his snooker even though he was absolutely useless at it. He always wanted to play for money, a pound or something like that.'

Alan Wilkins remembers visiting a betting shop with him during their apprentice days. 'He took me into this bookies, saying someone had told him about a horse. Giorgio was only on twelve pounds a week then but he put a tenner down on this horse. I couldn't believe it. It lost and I ended up lending him fifty pence so he could jump on a bus and see his mother to get some more money.'

Most of Chinaglia's salary – it jumped to twenty pounds a week when he signed as a professional – was disappearing in poker sessions and the betting shop. According to Vetch folklore, there was also an unpaid bill at the Continental Café, his favourite restaurant where he tucked into T-bone steaks. Here, Chinaglia was allowed a tab but he struggled to pay it off. His solution was to bet an entire week's wages on a horse. 'He was an incredible gambler,' recalls Roy Penny, an outside-right who was playing for the Swans on an amateur basis. 'It was cards first, horses second. I don't know where he got his money from. He used to go to the Langrove – a smart club on the outskirts of town which had a casino – and he owed quite a bit of money there. They used to let us have a slate because we were Swansea Town players. There was a story that Giorgio won a car in Cardiff. He was gambling, the other guy didn't have any money, so he took his car.'

For a night out, Black, Jones and Chinaglia would don their club blazers, embroidered with the Swansea Town crest, and frequent the Langrove. Recalls John Black, 'We went there one night. There were six of us – myself, Alan, Giorgio and three girls. We walked in and there was this bloke called Len who served us. He was a big Swansea fan and because we had the blazers on he was all over us. He was asking us about the last match and the next game.' The party of six ate its meal and listened to the cabaret. 'At the end of the night this Len character got the women their coats even though we hadn't paid or asked for the bill,' continues Black. 'We thought it was a freebie and left without paying. A couple of days later I'm running around the track at Skewen and Glyn Davies calls me over. "Oi! Come here, clever bastard!" His man-management skills were virtually nil. He shows me a letter from the Langrove together with a bill. It was something like ten or twelve pounds. I pulled Giorgio and Alan over. Alan starts saying, "I'm not paying a third because my girlfriend only had soup." We started arguing about who had what, but in the end we just paid it and had done with it.'

Friday nights on the town were strictly forbidden by the management, punishable with a hefty fine. But according to Dai Lawrence, a midfielder who played with Chinaglia in the 'A' team and also the Welsh League team, the Italian thought nothing of breaking this curfew, occasionally sneaking out of town to the Glen Ballroom in nearby Llanelli, a small town further west. 'It was a disco-cum-nightclub,' says Lawrence. 'One Friday night Giorgio went there with two other players – Alan Jones and Kenny Pound. They didn't get back until six in the morning and they had to play a game later that day.'

During the 1965–66 season Chinaglia became good friends with Roy Penny. He gravitated towards Penny because he shared a couple of his interests, namely cards and nightclubs. 'Giorgio was terrible with women', says Penny. 'Once he pulled a girl in St Benedict's – St Benedict's was a church that had been turned into a disco – and he took her back to his flat in the Uplands. Every 10 minutes we sent a taxi to his flat and watched what happened from the other side of the road. The drivers would knock on his door and he'd come out shouting and swearing. I thought he was going to kill one of the drivers. He knew it was me calling the taxis and the next morning, when we were all down the Vetch, he chased me around the ground and threw a pitchfork at me! That's the way he was.'

Most evenings Penny and Chinaglia went drinking together. Chinaglia would wear a long coat, black with padded shoulders, with a white scarf looped around his neck. In the no-nonsense drinking holes of Swansea, the dapper outfit had an inflammatory effect. As Penny discovered, his Italian mate was a magnet for trouble. 'Giorgio was a swine. He'd say, "Let's go to this pub" and we'd say, "OK, let's go." But there was always a reason why he wanted to go to that particular pub and nearly always it was to do with women. One night he wanted to go to The Tenby, which was a rough pub, a very rough pub. It had an iffy reputation in the town. There were four of us – myself, Giorgio and two friends of mine. We ended up pulling Giorgio out. I don't know what was going on but my mate dragged him out. I think it was over a woman. If he stayed I know there would have been big trouble. I wouldn't say he was big-headed but he had this aura about him. We ran away from quite a few places, to be honest. That was the other problem he had. People knew who he was, they'd make a bee-line for him and try and upset him. He was a big lad but he wasn't the best fighter in the world!'

His ability to cause a scene started in his days as an apprentice. Bill Edwards remembers an incident on a ferry from Holland, after Swansea played in a youth tournament in Amsterdam. 'Giorgio had had a few drinks and the next thing I knew he started performing,' says Edwards. 'There was this Norwegian fella with his girlfriend and Giorgio fancied the girl. He was on the deck of the boat, making fists and shouting at the Norwegian, "I'll fight him! I'll fight him!" I went over to Giorgio, who was a bit drunk, and said, "With your hands like that you'll get murdered. Don't spoil the trip."'

Glyn Davies decided to take a look at Chinaglia in a series of pre-season friendlies which were scheduled for August. The club arranged to play Newport County (twice), Merthyr Tydfil and Cheltenham Town over a week-long period. For the first, a 2–0 win against Newport at Somerton Park, Chinaglia came on as a second-half substitute. For the second, against Southern League side Merthyr Tydfil, at Penydarren Park, he played from the start and enjoyed an outstanding match, scoring twice in Swansea's 3–2 win. That summer evening the Merthyr line-up included Les Harris, Chinaglia's former team-mate at the Vetch. 'If he had his back to the defender Giorgio would try and flick it past him, or try and turn him,' says Harris. 'Looking back, he was technically better than most other players. In those days, it was all about running and workrate. There was a great emphasis on athleticism, but Giorgio was different. He always stood out because he was trying to do a lot on the ball.'

The headline in the *Evening Post* the following day was 'CHINAGLIA WAS SWANS STAR IN MERTHYR GAME'. The newspaper's match report was effusive. 'Chinaglia strolled through the match with the confidence and composure of a veteran. He scored two brilliant goals, crashed the ball against the crossbar with a tremendous 30-yard drive, and led the Merthyr defence a merry dance throughout. On this form, he must surely be in with a chance of a first-team spot next season.' Chinaglia had done enough to convince Davies that he was first-team material and was not picked for the final two friendly matches, against Cheltenham Town and the return game with Newport. 'Almost certainly,' remarks Gary Owen, 'I thought Giorgio was going to be a big star at the Vetch.'

On the eve of the new season, dressing-room morale was slightly subdued. The new manager's obsession with tactics had not impressed his players. Brian Evans, a talented and quietly-spoken winger who would play six times for Wales, says, 'Glyn and Tommy had different ideas. They would go on these coaching courses to Lilleshall and try to impose the things they learned there at Swansea.'

One of their theories angered the normally placid Ivor Allchurch.

'We were training at Skewen and they were trying to work out a system to beat the world,' explains John Black. 'Tommy put sand down the middle of the pitch and told Ivor, who was an inside-left, not to cross the line of sand. How could you tell Ivor, a world-class player, something like that. He said, "This is a joke!" and walked off.'

Roy Penny also remembers the incident. 'It was unusual because Ivor was a gentleman. The other pros also questioned it. But Giorgio was happy with it because it meant he didn't have to run far!'

The Swans began their 1965–66 campaign against Southend United at Roots Hall. Chinaglia was not involved in the 2–0 defeat. The second match of the season, three days later, was again away from home, at Bournemouth's Dean Court. This time Chinaglia did play, picked at inside-right to replace Derek Draper who had picked up an injury during the Southend match. The Italian did not prevent a second successive defeat although that evening, on the lush Dean Court surface, he scored Swansea's first goal of the season. For the Italian it was his first, and last, goal in English football.

It was a dramatic match, decided in the last few minutes. On a personal level, the 19-year-old Italian produced a decent performance. 'Bright star in the Swansea attack,' said the *Evening Post*, 'was Italian-born Giorgio Chinaglia, an inside-right of great potential.' There was praise, too, from the *Western Mail*. 'The Italian boy did well.' Chinaglia was the brains behind Swansea's first attack, providing a superb pass for Willie Humphries, but the Irishman failed to take advantage. Chinaglia himself came close to opening the scoring on two occasions. First, he headed Herbie Williams' cross over the bar, then he saw his fierce shot saved by Bournemouth's impressive goalkeeper, David Best. Chinaglia and Best would meet again in a notorious UEFA Cup match eight years later when the former was playing for Lazio and the latter for Ipswich Town.

In the second half, and with 20 minutes remaining, the home side took the lead through wing-half Ron Bolton but with three minutes left Chinaglia looked to have earned the Swans a point with a superbly taken goal. Kenny Pound, playing on the left wing, put the Italian clean through. He kept his nerve and placed the ball past Best. The Swansea fans in the crowd – most of them holidaymakers – were still cheering when, less than a minute later, forward John Archer hit Bournemouth's winner. 'We should have had a point,' said Davies after the final whistle. 'We had to pay dearly for some inexperience.' The Swansea players were still caught up in the euphoria of Chinaglia's superb equaliser when Bournemouth scored their second goal.

The Chinaglia at Bournemouth was vastly different to the one who laboured against Portsmouth during the Trevor Morris era. He was lively, dangerous and, aside from Allchurch, was Swansea's most impressive player. 'I believe that Chinaglia's bustling style and snap-shooting might well get him more success than many anticipate,' enthused sports writer Bill Paton in his regular look at the Vetch scene.

The 18-year-old Chinaglia injured his back at Dean Court and missed the game the following Saturday, at home to Swindon Town. Chinaglia recalls how Davies tried to make him play despite his injury. 'I had a bad back and I told him. He said, "Get on the field!" I could hardly run. He was an ignorant person. He didn't know how to communicate. He was always right.' Chinaglia finally won the argument and did not feature in the 1–1 draw. He was also absent from the side that was thumped 5–0 at Shrewsbury, the first in a series of horrible results that season.

'Giorgio was OK when I first arrived,' explains Davies, who soon fell out with the player and – somewhat inevitably – his father. 'Giorgio had a good physique which could be worked on. He needed time. He was a player of potential. In 12 to 18 months, he could have been a player of quality. There were a number of young players there with potential, but potential is not what you need when you're trying to stabilise a club in the lower divisions after a bad season. I put Giorgio in the first team, gave him a bit of a run, and, as I said, he looked promising. But he needed help and bringing along.'

After the Shrewsbury debacle, the manager wielded the axe for the following game, against Grimsby Town at the Vetch. There were eight changes – 'the biggest upheaval in years', said the Evening Post. One of them saw Chinaglia, playing well for the reserves, recalled at inside-right. Another of the new faces was John Roberts who was picked at centre-forward. 'On the Friday before the game,' says John Black, 'Glyn Davies knocked on my door and asked me if I knew where Giorgio lived. I said I did. He wanted me to take him there because he wanted to tell Giorgio he would be playing against Grimsby. He knew Giorgio lived in Uplands but didn't know what his exact address was. I took him to his bedsit and he answered the door while a girl was diving under the covers. I think Glyn knew somebody was in there with him but I don't think he sussed out what was going on.'

On an overcast afternoon in South Wales, the Swans notched up their first victory of the season, thanks to a 72nd-minute header from Allchurch. Grimsby were stubborn opponents and should have taken the lead after an hour but their forward, Rodney Green, missed a penalty. Chinaglia had a quiet game, his only real contribution coming midway in the first half, combining wonderfully with Roberts to send Allchurch racing clear, but the veteran fired his shot wide. 'Chinaglia,' wrote Bill Paton in the *Evening Post* the following Monday, 'will become a more penetrative and dangerous forward when he speeds up his game.'

He kept his place for the next match, a Tuesday-night fixture at home to Workington Town. Naturally, Davies was reluctant to tinker with the side after gaining that first victory. Workington, a club that broke into the league in 1951 and would eventually be replaced by Wimbledon in 1977, were bottom of Division Two with two points from four games. Swansea were just above them with three points but had played one game more. After this encounter the two clubs switched places.

In a match still remembered with shame at the Vetch, Workington thrashed the home side 6–1. It was Swansea's heaviest defeat since 1946. For once, Chinaglia must have wished he had not been picked. 'I remember watching it from the stands,' recalls Geoff Thomas. 'I was sitting with Derek Draper. I noticed that two of the Workington players had different coloured socks on. The club was struggling financially. I said to Derek, "This is a Mickey Mouse side." And they ended up putting six past us!' The man who inflicted most of the damage that night was Kit Napier, a fast and clever forward who had played for Preston in the 1964 FA Cup final. Napier scored a hat-trick as Workington, to a backdrop of slow handclapping from the angry home supporters, tore the Swansea defence to shreds. 'As for the Swansea forward line,' wrote Bill Paton, 'it was almost innocuous . . . teenagers Chinaglia and Roberts were out of their depth and are not ready for the hurly-burly of League football.' Workington were 4–0 up at half-time. Continued Paton, 'Had they run into double figures no one could have grumbled.'

When, during the interval, an announcement was made on the public address system regarding Swansea's next home fixture, a League Cup clash with Aston Villa, it was drowned out with booing. Through-out the second half the home fans vented their disapproval by sarcastically chanting 'Workington! Workington!' When they were five goals down, Willie Humphries scored Swansea's only goal with barely quarter of an hour left. Chinaglia had a wretched 90 minutes but so too did the rest of the Swansea team, even Ivor Allchurch. 'It was an absolute nightmare,' says John Black, who kept goal for the Swans that night. 'It was one of those games where everything they did came off. It was unbelievable.'

Among the 8,285 crowd that evening was 14-year-old Steve Hamer. A lifelong fan of the Swans, Hamer would become the club's chairman in 1996. 'We were an established Second Division club and had reached the semi-finals of the FA Cup the year before, and this little miners' village in Cumbria comes down and wipes the floor with us,' says Hamer. 'We were dreadful, absolutely dire. Giorgio's biggest contribution was taking part in the kick off every time Workington had scored. He kicked-off six times, I can still see him doing it today.' He saw several of Chinaglia's performances but was unimpressed. 'There was this Italian mystique in Britain at the time, John Charles had been at Juventus and there was Eddie Firmani, and Gigi Peronace. It was almost as if we were willing this young boy to be a genius. He wasn't bad with his back to goal but he didn't turn quickly and had no pace whatsoever.'

Heads rolled after the game and one of them was Chinaglia's. 'Not long after playing Workington we had a few games up north,' continues Black. 'We had to play at York and then go to Workington and Glyn didn't take some of the lads who had played in that 6–1 defeat. I was one and Giorgio was another. We were left behind in Swansea and on the night of the York match – which was in midweek – we went to the Park Hotel for a drink and to listen to a group, The Fireflies. Suddenly this group stops playing and someone announces the Swansea result – "York five, Swansea nil." And we cheered! I thought at the time we shouldn't be cheering but we were so peeved at being dropped.'

Chinaglia was relegated to the reserves after the Workington débâcle. Although he did not know it then, he would never start a first-team game for Swansea Town again.

CHAPTER SIX

IT HAD JUST GONE 9 A.M. when Keith Todd arrived at the Vetch Field. Usually the players rolled in an hour later but Todd turned up early because he needed treatment for a groin injury. He walked into the dressing-room to change and saw a sight he would always remember – Chinaglia, wearing his everyday clothes, lying motionless on one of the wooden benches. 'I looked at him and thought he was dead,' says Todd. He gave the teenager a poke and called his name. 'Then he woke up, got on his feet and left. Apparently he'd been up all night. I don't know how he got into the dressing-room. The cleaning lady had keys so I suppose she must have opened it. I don't know how long he'd been there. It wasn't the attitude of a professional footballer.'

This encounter occurred midway through the 1965–66 season when Chinaglia was out of the first-team reckoning. Feeling he was being unfairly treated by the management, he had completely lost interest in Swansea Town. The Swans, minus Chinaglia, suffered some heavy defeats. The 5–0 drubbing at York was followed by another massacre at the hands of Workington, this time a 7–0 thrashing at Borough Park. Glyn Davies was not prepared to give him a second chance. Asked why Chinaglia was kept simmering in the reserves, Davies answers, 'I put him in the first team just to educate him, get him used to the pace. Because he was young he hadn't developed the subtleties of the game, like cushioning balls, holding the ball, setting up other players.'

Back in Cardiff, in the Bamboo Room, Chinaglia's father was cursing Glyn Davies every night. 'Why he no play Giorgio?' he would exclaim to his regular customers. 'Giorgio score goals!' Week after week, the fraught restaurant-owner would call Peter Jackson, football correspondent on the *South Wales Echo*, Cardiff's evening newspaper, to lament his son's predicament. 'I didn't really know the man,' recalls Jackson, 'but he'd ring me up and say, "Why my son no play?" and "He [Glyn Davies] treat him badly".' Mario Chinaglia threatened to drive down to the Vetch with his meat cleaver. 'That manager, Glyn Davies,' he once told Geoff Thomas, who was visiting the restaurant, 'I'm going to go down there and cut his head off!'

Chinaglia's exile from the first team left many fans bemused. Results continued to be poor and the Swans were struggling to score goals. After the first 10 matches, the team was in last place with 30 goals conceded and eight goals scored. 'Ivor Allchurch used to tell Glyn Davies that I should be playing,' says Chinaglia. 'Glyn used to say to him, "I'm the manager!" Ivor was nice to me. "You're going to have a great career. Believe me, I know skilful players. You're going to have a great career," he would tell me.'

As the Swans fell to the foot of the table the *Evening Post* received hundreds of letters from irate supporters, usually listing who should be in the team, who should be dropped. 'I remember seeing one letter,' says John Black, 'and Giorgio's name was mentioned as one of the players who should have been playing.'

According to Geoff Thomas, Chinaglia was not Davies' type of player. 'Basically, Glyn liked players tackling and throwing themselves into places. Giorgio wasn't that type. I think that's the reason Glyn didn't like him. A couple of balls would go into the box and Giorgio wouldn't go for them. At the end of the day Glyn decided this guy wasn't good enough. A lot of players have been let go and gone on to make it elsewhere. He was just one of many who slipped through the net.'

Sensing his career at the Welsh club was over, and with his contract up at the end of the season, Chinaglia's behaviour – never exemplary at the Vetch – declined alarmingly. His biggest offence was to arrive late for training. The sessions started at Skewen at 10 a.m. prompt but Chinaglia, his shoulders stooped, would amble in at 10.15 a.m. or 10.30 a.m. Sometimes he would not appear. 'Giorgio was late pretty regularly,' recalls Thomas. 'Every three or four days. Sometimes he'd turn up at a crazy time like 11 a.m. He'd get changed and join in when we were well into our training.'

The demoralised Italian would sometimes turn to Thomas and say, 'I'm not gonna make it down here. They're not giving me a chance.' Thomas would reply, 'Well, don't be late for training. They don't like that sort of thing.' The advice was not heeded. 'He had it in his mind that he wasn't going to make it,' says Thomas.

In his last months at Swansea, the teenager channelled his energy into his nocturnal activities – playing cards and romancing women. 'In those days it was the rule that you weren't allowed to go out on a Thursday or Friday before a game. No drinking, no nightclubbing, nothing like that,' says Alan Jones. 'A few of us were 18 or 19 and we liked a pint but we stuck to the rule. But Giorgio was a law unto himself. He wasn't a big drinker but he liked to play cards. There was this gambling place in St Helens Road, near the Vetch Field, and he used to go there. Giorgio liked Swansea and he liked the women here as well. I remember calling on him on the way to the ground. We were playing in a match – I think it was a reserve game or Welsh League. I was all dressed and ready to play. I knocked on his door and he was in bed with his girlfriend! He made it down to the ground eventually.'

There is little doubt Davies and Casey were unaware of the extent of Chinaglia's off-the-pitch activities. His poor punctuality record was blamed on his reputation as a heavy sleeper. Had they known the truth, Chinaglia would probably have been sacked. 'Giorgio spent one Friday night at a pub called The Clarence,' recalls Roy Penny. 'He woke up in the afternoon, at about 2 p.m., and ran over to the ground because there was a game.' The Clarence Inn, a popular haunt for the players, was directly opposite the ground. 'We'd go to a nightclub, then go back there for a drink and play cards in the back room. Giorgio used to sleep on a bench inside. The landlady used to let us sleep there and she made us breakfast in the mornings.'

Glyn Davies punished Chinaglia for arriving late for training. He decided to hit Chinaglia in the pocket and fined him. The amounts varied depending on the gravity of the offence. 'Glyn Davies called me in once,' recalls Chinaglia. 'He said, "I'm fining you one pound and one shilling for being late." He said I turned up at 10.07 a.m. and training starts at 10 a.m. He even took the shilling from me.' Chinaglia was also fined for making what the manager called sarcastic remarks. 'In one game – I can't remember who it was against – I scored five goals. I told Glyn Davies that the same team drew 1–1 with our first team in a Welsh Cup tie a couple of weeks ago. He fined me fifty pence! In those days you could have lunch and dinner for fifty pence.'

According to Gordon Daniels, fining Chinaglia killed off any chance of a reconciliation between player and club. 'Things went from bad to worse. He became very dissatisfied. To be fair, Glyn Davies was very inexperienced as a football manager and Giorgio represented a problem that he couldn't cope with. Glyn introduced a purely disciplinarian approach, he didn't try to coax the boy. It was a heavy-handed approach and I didn't think it was the right one. Whether the softly-softly approach would have been any different we will never know.'

Davies insists the fines were a last resort and that he did 'try to put an arm around his shoulder'. All to no avail. 'We tried to encourage him, Tommy and myself. We couldn't have done much more. He was too close to his father. His father was determined to get him to Italy one way or the other and Italian fathers tend to dominate their sons. The die was cast before I got to Swansea. Giorgio was always doing smart-alec things. He thought he was clever by turning up for training late. When you're trying to organise a training session and you're trying to split players into groups, it's not easy when one is turning up late. We had to send apprentices to the digs to get him out of bed. I used to go ballistic with him.' Chinaglia's response was to merely shrug his broad shoulders and shout a retort in Italian. 'He was doing things that were not conducive to a successful side,' continues Davies. 'He'd dispute everything – who was taking the corners, who was taking the free-kicks. He was always moaning. You name it, he would moan about it. He used to make a nuisance of himself, not just to me but to Tommy and the other players. It was clear he didn't want to be at the Vetch.'

Davies had a one-to-one with Chinaglia soon after arriving from Yeovil. The forward confided that he felt he was never given a proper chance under Trevor Morris and wanted to play in the first team. Under Davies, Chinaglia responded well to the gruelling pre-season training sessions and found himself in serious contention for a first-team place. But by Christmas, as he continued to bait the manager, Chinaglia was back in the reserves or, humiliatingly, in the 'A' team.

'He wanted to kick authority in the face,' adds Davies. 'We tried to pull him into line. We threatened him, we played him in the third team, we fined him. We fined him just enough to hit him in the pocket. It was a totally sad affair but I inherited the situation.'

The fines had no effect because he could call on his parents for extra cash. His father ran a successful business and the Chinaglias were not short of money. 'When Glyn fined Giorgio,' recalls Geoff Thomas, 'he would just get on the phone to his mam. "Mam, can you send me some money?" I lost count of the number of times I was in a phone box with him and he'd ring home for money. I can hear him now. "Mam, mam. Can you send me a fiver?" They'd send him a letter with a fiver or tenner inside.'

He would also borrow from his friends. 'We used to lend him a couple of quid,' says Roy Penny. 'He was fined regularly and that's what really pissed him off.' The player also counted on the support of his fellow Italians. There was the tab at the Continental Café and an ice-cream peddler provided him with free ice-cream. 'He loved his ice-cream,' recalls Gordon Daniels. 'He had a typical Italian taste for ice-cream.'

His disputes with the management made him a cult figure with the new wave of apprentices. David Gwyther was one of the youngsters who noticed the rebellious Italian. 'We used to think he was a hell of a boy because he would stay out late with his mates or with a bird,' says ex-striker Gwyther. 'He used to smoke as well. I'd be sweeping the stand and I'd catch him having a sly fag. He was always getting into trouble. He'd be late for training in the morning so he had to do a bit extra in the afternoon. We'd be sweeping the stand or cleaning boots and there was Giorgio lapping around the ground on his own. It was very unusual for a player to turn up late for training unless they had a genuine excuse but Giorgio made a habit of it.'

Chinaglia had some titanic arguments with the fitness-mad Tommy Casey who demanded nothing less than 100 per cent from his players. 'He and Giorgio nearly came to blows a few times,' reveals Keith Todd. 'Tommy used to go spare with him because he wouldn't lift a leg. They used to argue in the dressing-room before we even got started. Giorgio was headstrong. If he didn't want to do something he wouldn't do it. It was always the same old thing – Giorgio wouldn't train and Tommy wanted him to train harder. It was a clash of personalities. I think Tommy gave up on him in the end.'

There was more. 'The arrival of Tom Hudson probably killed Giorgio off,' says John Roberts. 'Tom was a sports manager at Swansea University and Glyn Davies brought him to the Vetch to get us fit. He used to make us run to the Mumbles on the beach and run back through the sea. That would have helped see Giorgio off.'

Roy Penny remembers one argument between Casey and Chinaglia, one Thursday afternoon at the Skewen training ground. 'Tommy said to him, "Why don't you get off your arse and train?" They were in the middle of the pitch and they actually started pushing each other. It nearly came to a fight situation but it just fizzled out in the end. I thought they were going to come to blows.'

Casey, a human dynamo during his playing days with Leeds United, Newcastle United, Portsmouth and Bristol City, admits he was shocked by the forward's contempt for training. 'All I wanted to be in life was a professional footballer,' says Casey. 'I expected other players to have the same enthusiasm as I did. I couldn't believe players like Giorgio. Why do you want to be involved in the game if you don't want to participate? He was lazy. He ran only when he wanted to run. He was last at everything. I was always shouting "Catch up!" to him. He turned up only when he wanted to turn up and you can't do that when you're part of a group.'

Casey left East Belfast for Leeds in 1949 but it was at Newcastle, the club he joined in 1952, where he made a name for himself as a tough-tackling wing-half. He also played for Northern Ireland in their heroic World Cup campaign in 1958, in Sweden, when they reached the quarter-finals. He was player-manager of Gloucester City when he was invited to become trainer at the Vetch. Casey cannot recall any specific bust-ups with Chinaglia, but adds, 'He was such a volatile lad. You couldn't tell him anything. I always had to fight my way through life but in my opinion he was spoiled at a very young age. I think there was money in the family.'

Glyn Davies knew Casey from his Derby County days and saw him as the ideal right-hand man. 'Two assets a player needed to play for Tommy,' explains David Ward, 'were a good pair of legs and a strong pair of lungs. If you did enough running, tackling and chasing back then you were half-way there. But that was never Giorgio's style. He would flick a ball over a defender's head and that was totally alien to Tommy's philosophy. He wanted 99 per cent graft and one per cent talent.' The rows between Chinaglia and Casey became a daily feature of Vetch life. The coach would order him to run to the Mumbles and back. Chinaglia, insisting he was fit enough, would shout back, 'I score goals!' It fell on deaf ears and Chinaglia, at his own, meandering pace, would start to jog along Mumbles Road, his eyes peeled for the first passing milk float.

'Everybody had run-ins with Tommy, not just Giorgio,' adds Ward. 'His style was very, very abrasive and he had set ideas on how the game should be played. They came up with this 4-2-4 system with man-marking and everyone was given a task to do. If they didn't do those tasks he'd shout and scream from the touchline. I remember him screaming at Giorgio for not chasing back and not marking the opposition's number nine at corners. Tommy tended to find faults with most players.'

Casey believes Chinaglia's poor attitude was down to the heedlessness of youth. 'He had the ability but not the gumption to go with it,' he explains. 'He was just a young playboy, a bit like George Best. He was a very temperamental lad. He just wanted to do what he wanted to do, not what those above him wanted him to do. At the time he was a young lad and when you're that age you think you know everything. I know he liked to stay out late but if you're a professional athlete you can't go out drinking and chasing women. We'd all love to do that but you have to decide whether you want that or football.'

The one aspect of Chinaglia's game which infuriated the trainer was his selfishness, a refusal to be a team player. 'He was all flamboyance,' says Casey. 'He wanted to take six players on and stick the ball into the net. It wasn't enough to get the ball and pass it to someone himself.' Chinaglia would never lose that egocentric streak. At Lazio he continually told his fellow players, '*Passala la palla! Se tu mi passi la palla io faccio gol!*' – Pass me the ball! If you pass me the ball I score goals! Adds Casey, 'Everything had to be flamboyant. I didn't mind him taking on six players if he had the ability to do that but he didn't. He thought he was a better player than he was.'

As an inside-forward, Chinaglia's brief was to get from one penalty box to the other. 'He didn't want to do that. All he wanted was self-glory,' says Casey. 'He was a show-off. He'd try and take on as many players as he could but he'd lose the ball and then we'd be exposed at the back because the other players were out of position. He wasn't a good team player. He was very greedy on the ball. If you're greedy, then you have to be a very good player so you don't lose possession. Giorgio would dribble past two or three players, lose possession and then just stand around. But it's a team game. You need ability but you must play for the rest of the team, which means working.'

In October 1965, Mario Chinaglia paid another visit to the Vetch. He had 'certain proposals to make' to the manager. Top of his agenda was buying out his son's contract so he would be free to play for an Italian club. On this occasion, Chinaglia senior took with him one of his burly Italian friends. Keith Todd remembers the Wednesday the duo dropped in at the ground. 'They were both wearing long coats and were standing outside Glyn's office. It was like the Mafia had come down! I didn't know who it was at first. Then I found out it was Giorgio's father.'

Davies took umbrage at Chinaglia arriving with company and agreed to a meeting only if it was between manager and father. 'His father's friend was a bit of a gorilla,' recalls Davies. 'I said to the gorilla, "You wait outside. This has got nothing to do with you. I'll talk about this only with Giorgio's father." He came into the office and started telling me what he wanted and what he didn't want. He was quite aggressive and raised his voice to make a point. He wanted something for himself and something extra for Giorgio.'

According to Andrea Delnero, Mario Chinaglia wanted two thousand pounds. 'When he found out Giorgio was in the first team he said, "I'm going to see Swansea because they had my boy for nothing",' recalls Delnero. The restaurateur asked Davies for the money, threatening, 'If you don't give it to me I'll take my son away.'

Bill Edwards says the manager's response was equally forthright. 'He told Giorgio's father, "You can go and you can take your son with you." He had no intention of releasing Chinaglia. Davies had no money to buy new players and might need the youngster in case of injuries. And if another club wanted to buy him, Swansea could make money on the 18 year old. Because of his age and undoubted natural ability, he was valued in the ten thousand pound bracket. As an apprentice he had cost the Swans nothing bar wages. 'I had enough on my plate without his father coming down,' says Davies. 'I wasn't happy because the last thing I wanted to do was argue with people.'

Roy Penny says the player was unhappy about his father driving down to see the manager. 'Giorgio wasn't pleased about that. He felt he was a grown man and that his father shouldn't do those sort of things. He felt embarrassed.'

Even though eight months remained on his contract, Chinaglia's career with Swansea Town effectively ended that October afternoon. 'After that meeting with his father Giorgio just went through the motions,' explains Davies. 'He didn't bother. He was staying up late around the town. Tommy and I kept an eye on him at the club but we couldn't control him at night. With his father's determination to get him over to Italy, it was a question of when it was going to happen, not if.'

For reserve and Welsh League away games, Chinaglia did not turn up at the pick-up point at the arranged time. 'He'd keep us waiting in the bus for half an hour,' says David Ward. 'Then we'd see him ambling down the street. On some occasions he wouldn't turn up at all. Most of the players got pissed off with him. Some of the younger players found it funny – "Oh look, Giorgio's late again!" – but it wore thin with them as well.'

With most of his modest salary dissipated by fines, and the money from his parents covering the five-pound rent, Chinaglia resorted to stealing milk from the doorsteps of Swansea's terraced homes for his breakfast. 'He would walk along Richardson Street – the road that led to the players' entrance – in the early hours and help himself to a pint of milk,' says David Ward. 'That was the stage it got to. He did it on a number of occasions. The milkman had just been, people hadn't taken their milk in and it was too good an opportunity to miss.'

His financial predicament was not helped in January when he was fined five pounds, not by Glyn Davies but by Swansea Magistrates' Court for riding his Lambretta without a licence and insurance. He was giving his friend Mario Maccarinelli a ride home when police stopped them. 'Giorgio said to the policeman, "I am Giorgio Chinaglia." The policeman said, "I don't give a damn who you are, I'm booking you."'

During this unhappy spell he showed glimpses of the talent which had convinced Trevor Morris to sign him nearly four years previously. In a reserve match against Ferndale, which the Swans won 3–0, Chinaglia opened the scoring with a powerful shot outside the area after beating two defenders. He then hit the crossbar with a 25-yard shot before setting up the third goal, scored by his close friend, Ken Pound. 'One minute he looked awkward, the next he would do something out of the ordinary,' recalls David Gwyther. 'I was a forward as well, that's why I took an interest in him. He was capable of doing things and scoring unusual goals. I remember watching him once – I think it was in a Welsh League match – and he did nothing throughout the game. Then he whacked one in from a tight angle.'

Gary Owen, who lived in the suburb of Mount Pleasant, not far from Chinaglia's bedsit in the Uplands, occasionally walked home with the Italian after training. 'I can remember him saying to me, "I know I'm going to be a big star." And this was when he was really doing badly at Swansea. It was laughable really because he wasn't anywhere near the first team.'

The forward would repeat this mantra to Mario Maccarinelli. 'He used to tell me and my wife, "One day you are going to beg for my autograph because I'm going to be a goldie!" I used to say, "Come off it, Giorgio." And then he'd say, "Don't worry, you will beg for my autograph." All the Italians used to go and watch him play. He was happy with the Italians because we made him feel a star.'

Almost six months after his last league appearance, Chinaglia found himself back in the first team. Davies named him as a substitute for the critical home match against third-from-bottom Brentford. Keith Todd, although fit to play, had been troubled with a leg injury and Davies, wary Todd may not last the distance, wanted another striker on stand-by.

That March afternoon Chinaglia's already strained relationship with the club reached its nadir when he demonstrated just how apathetic he was to the Swansea cause. For a 3 p.m. Saturday kick-off, the players reported to the Vetch no later than 2 p.m. but by 2.30 p.m. Chinaglia had not turned up. 'We were all dressed in our kit and ready to go out,' recalls Brian Evans, 'but there was no sign of Giorgio.'

Two of the players against Brentford – Geoff Thomas and Alan Jones – remember the scenes in the dressing-room as kick-off approached. 'The club was making phone calls to find out where he was and Glyn was walking around shouting, "Where is he? Where is he?" There was a major panic on,' says Thomas. Apprentices were even dispatched to Chinaglia's bedsit at Glanmor Road, with orders to drag him to the ground. Then, 10 minutes before kick-off, he shuffled into the dressing-room, unshaven and wearing his overcoat. 'He looked like death warmed up,' adds Thomas. 'I thought to myself, "Fuckin' hell!" All the players were looking at each other, saying, "I wasn't with him last night".'

Brian Evans adds, 'It was the first time I'd seen anything like that, turning up just before the kick-off. Glyn went berserk with Giorgio.' Casey added his voice to the angry chorus. 'I can't take much more of you!' he shouted at the disinterested forward. 'After that the writing was on the wall,' says Thomas. 'Late for training was bad enough but late for a game, especially that late!'

The reason for Chinaglia's absence? 'I remember him telling me he'd been gambling until five or six in the morning or something like that,' replies Jones. 'I know he was up until very late. He'd gone home, went to bed and crashed out. Next thing he knows it's 2 p.m. He puts his clothes on and runs down to the ground.' Despite his condition Chinaglia made an appearance against the Londoners. With 20 minutes remaining, Davies was forced to throw him on to replace Ivor Allchurch, who hobbled off with an injury to his right knee. Swansea were 1–0 up at the time, thanks to a 51st minute goal scored by Jones, but four minutes after Chinaglia's arrival, Brentford equalised. John Regan, who signed for Brentford just days earlier from Shrewsbury Town, scored from close range.

The match ended 1–1 and Chinaglia, who made no impact in a drab game, had made his last first-team appearance for Swansea Town. 'When he played in the first team,' says Roy Penny, 'he did OK. He wasn't great but he did OK. I thought that would gee him up but I think he just wanted to get away.' Geoff Thomas blames the management for Chinaglia's disinterest. 'I think Giorgio sensed pretty early with Glyn that he wasn't going to be involved. The club was struggling in the Third Division and you've got a guy scoring goals in the reserves but not getting picked for the first team. Naturally, he sensed Glyn didn't like him.'

Chinaglia's last days at the Vetch were acrimonious. A week after arriving minutes before kick-off against Brentford, he failed to turn up for training. Davies, at the end off his tether, came down hard. No fine this time. Instead, two 14-day suspensions. The player was notified of his punishment by a letter in the post. 'I'll never kick another ball for Swansea,' said Chinaglia in the *Western Mail*, after learning of his suspension. He said he did not turn up for training because he felt unwell after a Welsh League match, against Newport-based side Lovell's Athletic. The club said he failed to provide a reason for his absence. 'I don't see eye-to-eye with the manager,' added Chinaglia, who spent his month-long exile with his family in Cardiff.

Mario Chinaglia became involved. 'My son will never go to Swansea again and I will make sure of that,' he told Pat Searle. 'My boy has never had a chance at Swansea. He's not going back.' But he did go back, reporting for training a month later. However, a divorce was unavoidable. Talking about his last few months at the Vetch, Chinaglia now recalls, 'I think it was about November time Glyn Davies said to me, "I'm going to get rid of you. You're useless." After that I didn't give a damn. I didn't care. I knew I wouldn't stay. I have no idea why he didn't like me.' He is critical of Davies' football philosophy. 'He said he was going to teach me to be a proper football player but he forgets about fantasy. Good players, you've got to let them have fantasy on the field, skill and intelligence. They liked the long ball at Swansea. They didn't like skill. It was the wrong mentality.'

Gordon Daniels, who often had the task of implementing Davies's punishments, says, 'I liked Giorgio very much. He was always polite and well-mannered. He had charm and charisma, no doubt about that. But he had this thing of not wanting to conform to rules and regulations. He was very young and immature. I don't know what upbringing he had in Cardiff but I imagine his father could be quite strict. When he came to Swansea he was let off the leash and quite possibly took advantage of that.'

Chinaglia's father, who had spent the last 18 months vowing to find his son an Italian club, appeared to have finally achieved that aim. Massese, a third division club in Massa, near Chinaglia's home town of Carrara, were interested in signing the teenager. 'I knew Giorgio was on his way to Italy,' says Thomas. 'I knew well before the end of the season because I remember him asking me how long it was before the season finished. "I'm going back home to Italy. My dad has sorted something out for me." That's what he told me.'

Alan Wilkins, who was playing for Lovell's Athletic at the time, received a call from Chinaglia senior which revealed how desperate he was for his son to leave Swansea. If Wilkins could convince Lovell's to sign him, not play him and then release him to an Italian club, he and his wife could have a two-week holiday in Italy, paid for by the restaurant-owner. 'He didn't want Giorgio to have any ties with Swansea,' says Wilkins. 'I said it was smashing to offer me that but there was no need. Giorgio would be a free agent in the summer and there was no point wasting his money.'

In a season that saw them lose 7–0 at Workington, 5–2 at Peterborough and 6–2 at QPR – 'When Glyn Davies came he had dark hair. After 18 months he had gone grey,' says Tommy Jackson – the Swans moved away from the relegation zone thanks to a decent late run that saw them collect eight points out of a possible ten. Davies's side finished five points above the relegation zone, in 17th place.

With his contract expiring on 30 June it came as no surprise when the club released Chinaglia on a free transfer. His departure was briefly mentioned in the *Evening Post*. In his back-page report of 26 May, Bill Paton wrote, 'Chinaglia made four first team appearances this season'. That was the extent of his Vetch Field 'obituary'. 'We knew he wouldn't accept a new contract so we released him,' explains Daniels. 'We had our pride after paying him throughout his apprenticeship, but since he hadn't really made it in the first team, since his father wanted him to go back to Italy and considering all the problems we had with him, we felt it wasn't worth our while trying to keep hold of him. We let him go and wished him luck. Best close the book. At the time we didn't feel we'd lost a great player.'

As far as the manager was concerned, he had got shot of his Latin troublemaker and his interfering papa. 'I'd got fed up of Giorgio as a person because he'd become a nuisance,' admits Davies. 'Whatever we tried to do didn't work. If we were a club with a lot of money we could have taken him to task but it's difficult when you haven't got money. His general attitude was wrong. It's no good quarrelling and having upsets and Giorgio developed this attitude. We were worried about his behaviour rubbing off. It's easier to follow a bad egg than a good one. In some respects. I wasn't happy to see him go because he had quality but in other respects I was glad because he had become a disruptive influence. There was no way he was going to stay in Swansea. We put him in the first team, gave him an opportunity early on, but to no avail.'

Many players believe Davies and Casey were to blame for the teenager's disillusionment, citing poor man-management and a failure to understand – and appreciate – Chinaglia's precocious talent. 'As a manager you've got to know every individual and treat them differently,' says Keith Todd. 'I don't think Glyn was very good at that. He wielded the stick and that doesn't always work. Giorgio was at Swansea at the wrong time and with the wrong manager. I'm glad he went on to prove his talent even though it wasn't with us.'

David Ward says he felt sorry for Chinaglia during that final season. 'He should have had a lot more counselling and direction. They were hitting him in his pocket rather than getting him into a room and trying to sort the problem out. Back then, there was no support from the manager, the directors or the secretary. Players were seen almost as a commodity. If we had problems we were on our own.'

Alan Jones also feels Davies handled the Chinaglia situation badly. 'You'll never get the best out of people if you have a go at them in front of others. Glyn had rows out in the open with Giorgio, in front of everybody. That's not the way to do it, is it? If he wanted to tell Giorgio something it should have been done in private. If someone had been on my back all the time there was no way I would have responded.'

Roy Penny is also scathing about how the club was run in the mid and late 1960s, claiming the atmosphere inside the dressing-room was poor. 'The players didn't have any respect for Glyn and we were all looking to get away from the Vetch. Giorgio made the break and he'll always be known as the one Swansea let go.'

At the time Chinaglia was given a free transfer, the club also released one of his contemporaries, left-back Tommy Jackson. 'Quite a few people, myself included, didn't know what Glyn wanted as far as players went,' says Jackson. 'I couldn't get on with him. He couldn't man-manage and he wasn't light-hearted. Had Trevor Morris stayed I'm sure Giorgio would have been in the first team within a couple of years. He knew how to coax him. It was no good shouting at him like Glyn did.

News of Chinaglia's move to Massese, along with a £10,000 signing-on fee, reached South Wales in late June, a week before his contract terminated. 'You know as much as we do about this reported move,' a baffled Gordon Daniels told Pat Searle. Trevor Wood, the club's vice-chairman, was also confused. 'Technically he cannot be transferred without our permission until 1 July.' Even thousands of miles away, Chinaglia was managing to cause Swansea Town grief.

There had been no interest in Chinaglia from British clubs. The forward later claimed Cardiff City and Hereford United had made enquiries but both were put off by the 'troublemaker' tag Swansea had given him. Richie Morgan signed for Cardiff the year Chinaglia was let go. He claims Cardiff, managed at the time by 'Iron Man' Jimmy Scoular, an abrasive, no-nonsense Scot, would not have been interested in signing him. 'He was seen as that Italian waster down the road,' says Morgan. 'Not even clubs like Merthyr, who traditionally took rejected players from the league, wanted him.'

There were several reasons for his failure at the Vetch. He looked mediocre when given a chance in the first team but the Welsh League, a poor substitute for the Combination, was not ideal preparation for league football. He was also unsuited to the hustle and bustle of the

English game and would not flourish under the abrasive pairing of Davies and Casey. His father was an unsettling influence, especially during his final year. 'Leaving Swansea was a blessing in disguise for him,' concludes Geoff Thomas. 'Look what would have happened if he had made it – he would have played in the Third and Fourth Divisions.'

Three years after leaving the Vetch, Chinaglia was one of the hottest properties in Italian football. Having been given away by Swansea Town, he joined Lazio in 1969 for a then-massive £140,000. 'I always thought he had a chance,' says Glyn Davies. 'What he achieved at Lazio didn't surprise me.' Davies's reign at Swansea came to an abrupt end five months after the Italian's departure. Two months into the 1966–67 season, and with just one win from the first nine games, Davies and Casey resigned. 'All Giorgio needed,' adds Davies, 'was discipline and direction.'

Gordon Daniels admits the free transfer in June 1966 has haunted the club ever since. 'We have regrets, no question about that. We're proud of the fact we brought him into league football but not proud of the fact he left us.' Daniels tried, unsuccessfully, to find Chinaglia in 1982 when Swansea were in serious financial trouble and Chinaglia was a millionaire playing for New York Cosmos. He wanted to propose that Chinaglia buy the club or lend it some money. 'Maybe if he'd been pushed into the first team a bit sooner we would've seen a hint of his superstardom,' says Daniels. 'We were so glad for him when he did well in Italy.'

As the 1960s went on, the club slid further down the league. Even if Chinaglia had been a first-team regular, he would have been playing in Division Four. 'The best thing they ever did,' he says, 'was give me a free transfer. It changed my life. I will always thank Swansea for that.'

CHAPTER SEVEN

FINDING HIS SON an Italian club had not been easy for Mario Chinaglia. During Giorgio's last weeks at Swansea Town he had been ringing Italian football journalists to ask if there were any openings at clubs who played in *Serie C* (Italy's equivalent of England's third division) or below. According to the rules of the *Federcalcio* (the Italian Football Federation) his son could not sign for a club in either *Serie A* or *Serie B* – those signed from a foreign league had to play in the third division for at least three years before they could join clubs in the top two divisions.

Having little luck with the journalists, Mario Chinaglia flew to Italy to find a club that would take his son. Naturally, he began his quest in his native province of Massa. The first club to show an interest in the Swansea forward was Marinella, one of Massa's minor clubs, based in Marina di Massa, the town's harbour area. Recalls Andrea Delnero, 'When Swansea wouldn't give him any money, Mario said, "I'm going to find him a team in Italy" and he did – Marinella. He came back to Cardiff and told Giorgio, "Right, you go there." When Giorgio arrived in Marina, he took one look at the place and caught the next plane home. He was back in Cardiff the next day! "I don't want to play there. They are not even in the fourth division," he said.'

Giorgio Chinaglia also tried his luck at Carrarese, the *Serie C* club based in his hometown, Carrara. 'Like Cardiff City,' says Delnero, 'they showed no interest. They said they already had too many players but they tried him.' The trial was not a pleasant experience. 'They gave him the wrong size boots. They didn't give him any shorts and he played with four people,' sighs Delnero. 'You can't tell if anyone is good when he's playing with four people. You have to play in a team.'

It was Delnero who fixed him up at Massese, Massa's flagship club which also played in *Serie C*. 'I was going to Italy myself and I thought I would give Massese a try,' he recalls. 'I went there on the coach and I talked to their manager and their people. I said, "I've known the boy since he was nine and he played in the kitchen because he is crazy about football. The boy is good. You have to try him. You won't be sorry." The manager said to me, "Yes, I believe you" and they tried him. They gave him the right boots, they dressed him right and they played him in a team.'

Impressed by Chinaglia's performance, Massese took him on and agreed to pay him £200 a month, plus an extra £30 for every point the team gained. 'And what happened?' smiles Delnero. 'His father went out there and wanted money. He liked the money, Mario.' Unlike Swansea, Massese agreed to his demands, paying him £6,000.

He spent the first four months living with his grandmother in Carrara and those early days were difficult. Chinaglia had left Italy when he was nine, grown up in Cardiff and revelled in the Swansea night-life – the clubs, the cards, and, of course, the women. The town of Massa, in the hills of north-west Tuscany, was vastly different – and for a 19-year-old boy, dull by comparison; old men playing cards outside bars, women in black staring in bemusement at Chinaglia's drainpipe trousers and shaggy haircut.

The biggest shock was *ritiro* – retreat – an intense period of training in complete isolation. Italian clubs would, and still do, take their players to a remote destination, usually in the mountains, for exhaustive pre-season training. Here they stayed, away from any distractions and living under strict curfews until the season started. In July Chinaglia and his team-mates were taken to Castelnuovo di

Garfagnana, a rural village, population less than 7,000, high in the Apuan Alps. This was home until September when the *Serie C* campaign kicked off. The players' diets were strictly controlled, they had to be in bed at 9 p.m. and fraternisation with the local female population was strictly forbidden. It was a far cry from Swansea's High Street.

Chinaglia, accustomed to finishing training at midday and socialising until the early hours of the morning, found *ritiro* destestable. He was to play in three Italians clubs and at every one he constantly told his team-mates of the difference between training in Britain and Italy.

'He said he used to have more free time at Swansea, more leisure time, more drinking time,' says Giuseppe Wilson, a defender who played with Chinaglia at Internapoli and Lazio. 'He said there wasn't as much pressure at Swansea.'

After only a few days at Castelnuovo di Garfagnana, Chinaglia packed his bags and fled back to South Wales. His father was furious but the player showed no signs of returning to Italy to 'the horror of that mountain retreat'. Three days after his return, the telephone rang at the Chinaglia family's house in Cardiff. It was Massese. 'They said come back,' recalled Chinaglia in an interview in 1973. He did go back. 'And do you know what those clever people did? They bought me a sports car.' A red Fiat to be precise. 'They said come back, and they bought me a sports car.'

Massese had played their trump card. Only a few months previously, Chinaglia had been stealing milk bottles for breakfast and, penniless after Swansea's fines, scrounging money off his mother. Now he was the owner of a £2,000 (the equivalent of £24,000 in the year 2000) car and there was the promise of more riches to come. 'They gave me a sports car and a lot of money. The homesickness soon goes away, believe you me,' says Chinaglia.

Back in Swansea, his team-mates and friends were unsure of Chinaglia's fate. After he was released by Glyn Davies, there were rumours he had returned to Italy but nothing was substantiated. One minute he was at the Vetch, the next he was gone. No goodbye, no farewell note. Says Roy Penny, 'I heard there had been words between Glyn and Giorgio and all of a sudden he'd gone.'

Alan Jones adds, 'I knew he had gone back to Italy but I didn't know what he was doing until he sent me a letter.' Jones received Chinaglia's letter later in the year, in the first week of November. 'I am sorry that I have not written earlier but I have never been the one for writing,' he explained. 'I am missing Swansea a bit. How are all the women treating you? Here we aren't even allowed to talk to women or girls. It's like a jail.' Chinaglia also sent Jones a newspaper cutting 'to show that I am doing well for a change'. He continued, 'I wish you were here because some of the players are hopeless.'

A few months into the 1966–67 season, while visiting his family in Cardiff, Chinaglia drove to Swansea to see his old friends. One of his stops was Alan Jones's house in the Townhill area. 'It was eight or nine months after he'd gone,' remembers Jones. 'He knocked on my door. I'll never, ever forget it. He was as straight as a ramrod. He was dressed in white trousers, white shirt, cravat and driving a white car. I'm sure it was an Alfa Romeo. The change in a man! He took me for a drive to see our old haunts. He frightened the life out of me with his driving. Typical Italian driver! I was glad to get out.'

Chinaglia scored his first goal for Massese in a friendly – the irony of it being against Lazio, his future club, was lost at the time – which ended 2–2. 'Before I arrived Massese were watched by 2,000 people. When I arrived that doubled,' boasts the striker. Then he experienced the two sides of *calcio*. After beating Carrarese 1–0 in the derby game, the players were each rewarded with a £50 bonus. But when they suffered their first defeat of the season, against Ravenna, which saw them fall from first to third, they were fined £15 'for not trying'. Chinaglia scored only five goals during the 1966–67 season, but his displays were impressive enough. Massese finished fourth, just missing out on promotion to *Serie B*. In the summer of 1967 he was summoned to do National Service. He would spend 18 months in army barracks in Rome.

Had he stayed in Britain, he would have been exempt from *servizio militare*. According to Salvatore Amodeo, the obligation to serve in the Italian Army made Chinaglia think hard about leaving Britain for a club there. 'He was worried about the military service. I told him, "Giorgio, if you do well for your club you will have an easy life when you're called up by the military." It didn't quite work out that way. After he did his National Service he came to Cardiff to see his family and he had a go at me. "Fuckin' military service wasn't as fuckin' easy as you said!" I remember those very words. He really chided me. "You lying bastard! You said I'd be a star in the army." I said to him, "Giorgio, I expected you to play a bit more before they called you up!"'

As a player Chinaglia had a far easier time in the army than ordinary citizens. Professional footballers doing National Service left their barracks on Thursday night and stayed with their clubs until the following Tuesday. This meant they only had to endure two days of the usual military chores. Despite the perks football brought, the army was not to Chinaglia's liking, as Alan Wilkins discovered when he met his old Italian friend during one of his visits to South Wales. 'When we were at Swansea we played on Boxing Day which meant we had to train Christmas morning. Anyway, the landlady of our digs was spending Christmas with her daughter in Port Talbot and she left me and Giorgio some cooked chicken for lunch. "You can do what you want with it," she told us. But we couldn't get the cooker to work so our Christmas dinner that year was cold chicken and cold tomato soup. When I saw Giorgio after he'd been in the Army he said, "Every night I cried myself to sleep. I could have had that chicken and tomato soup time and time again." That's how bad the food was in the Army.'

While he was fulfilling his military duty, Massese sold the striker to Internapoli, another *Serie C* outfit and Naples' second club. Wealthy and ambitious, they had just won promotion from the *quarto serie* (fourth division) and saw Chinaglia as their passport to *Serie B*. 'I remember the exact amount we bought him for,' says Gianni Di Marzio, Internapoli's assistant coach at the time. 'He cost us one hundred and eight million lire – around two hundred thousand pounds – which was an exorbitant fee at the time but he was a name in *Serie C*. He was one of the emerging names in the lower divisions and we went after him.'

Massese had made a huge profit. Chinaglia, too, was financially better off with the move south. Internapoli more than doubled his monthly salary, from £200 a week at Massese to £500 a week in Naples. On top of that came the bonuses, £150 for every goal scored and £50 for every point the team earned. 'There were rumours of him being a good player. When Chinaglia arrived he was physically knackered because he'd been doing National Service,' remembers Giuseppe Wilson.

Like Chinaglia, Wilson had a British connection. He was born in Darlington to an English father and an Italian mother. His father was a NATO official based at Bagnoli in southern Italy. His mother was Neapolitan and Wilson was raised in Naples, leaving Darlington when he was six months old, never to return. Chinaglia and he became close friends. They joined Lazio at the same time and at Tor di Quinto, Lazio's training ground, the pair were inseparable. 'We were friends but we were totally different men. The one thing we agreed on was football,' says Wilson, an intelligent and aggressive *libero*. 'Our lives ran parallel. We played in *Serie C* together, we played in the military team during National Service, we moved to Lazio together, we suffered at Lazio, we lost a championship together and won a championship together.'

Internapoli were coached by an eccentric Argentinian, Oscar Montes. It was rumoured that Omar Sivori, the former Juventus and Italy inside-forward who was playing for Napoli at the time, had got Montes the Internapoli job. His club had spent heavily in 1967, not just on Chinaglia but on a number of other players who had *Serie A* experience. 'Internapoli spent so much on Chinaglia because they wanted to be big,' says Di Marzio. 'They wanted the city to have another football club, to have a derby like they did in Genoa, Turin and Milan.

'At the start it didn't go too well for Giorgio,' adds Di Marzio. 'He wasn't scoring, the team wasn't doing too well and Montes was sacked.' Di Marzio briefly replaced Montes until a permanent successor could be found. In his first game in charge, at Chieti, a town near the Adriatic coast, Di Marzio watched in delight as Chinaglia, with just one goal to his name at the half-way point of the 1967–68 season, scored twice in a 2–0 win. 'That is the match I remember him most for. We played high in the mountains, on a pitch with no grass,' he says.

That match in the Abruzzo region was a turning point for the young forward who had been sarcastically nicknamed *Signor Cento Miliardi* – Mr One Hundred Million – by the *tifosi* unimpressed with the expensive new signing. He scored nine goals in the next ten games as Internapoli finished fourth in *Serie C*'s southern section (*Serie C* was split into three divisions – one for northern Italy, one for the central regions and one for the south). His sudden explosion had attracted the interest of five big fish – Milan, Inter, Bologna, Fiorentina and Lazio.

'I gave Chinaglia the number ten shirt to stop him being booed,' explains Di Marzio. 'The supporters had a tendency to criticise whoever wore the number nine shirt because they were the main forward who was expected to score. To relieve him of that burden, to stop him having psychological problems, I made him number ten even though he was our centre-forward. With the number ten jersey, he scored all the time!'

Chinaglia, like the rest of his colleagues, lived in an apartment right next to the Collana stadium, where Internapoli played, which stood in the Vomero district of Naples. Continues Di Marzio, 'Off the field he was a big baby, very generous, very genuine. I can't say anything but good things about him. If I had to criticise him, it's that he trusted too many people.' He is referring to his ill-fated spell as Lazio president in the early 1980s. 'He thought everyone around him was his friend. He couldn't see evil in people.'

Chinaglia became close to Di Marzio. 'When he joined Lazio he asked me to come over many times,' he says. It was through the coach that he met his first wife, Connie Eruzione, the daughter of an American NATO officer stationed in Naples. 'I knew the NATO people because I trained the youth players at their base. I was invited to one of their parties, I took Giorgio because we were good friends and it was at this party that he met Connie,' says the former coach. They eventually married in July 1970, at the city's San Vincenzo Pallotta church.

He ended his first year at Internapoli with a total of ten goals in 31 games, a modest tally, but he had shown promise since the Christmas break. Chinaglia did enough to attract the interest of two further clubs, the Milanese giants, Milan and Inter. Following Italy's disastrous World Cup campaign in England in 1966, when they were eliminated in the first round after losing to North Korea in Middlesbrough, the *Federcalcio* slapped a ban on foreign imports. Now the clubs had to scour the lower divisions for new talent, a blessing for young players such as Chinaglia.

The following season, under the eye of Internapoli's new coach, the Brazilian Luis Vinicio, he scored 14 goals in 35 appearances. According to Di Marzio, Chinaglia improved under Vinicio's tutorship. 'He learned a lot more from Vinicio. He was an ex-forward himself, a fantastic player.' Known as *O Leone* – the lion – Vinicio was *Serie A*'s top goalscorer in 1966 when he was playing for Vicenza. 'Giorgio was playing in exactly the same position Vinicio had played and he taught him everything that he knew. Giorgio knew his strengths. He had this progressive run. His speed increased the longer he ran and he had a right foot that was deadly. I had no doubts that he would be a great success. You could see what type of player he was. He wasn't refined, he was a forward like John Charles – a buffalo.'

Chinaglia continued to loathe training. 'He didn't like physical exercise,' recalls Di Marzio. 'He just wanted to play in mini-matches and he wanted to win those. If he didn't score he got upset.' In 1969 Chinaglia had served his three-year purgatory in *Serie C* and could now join a team in the top flight. Lazio swooped. The club's owner, Umberto Lenzini, a property developer born in Colorado, in the USA, paid Internapoli two hundred million lire – nearly four hundred thousand pounds – for their centre-forward. 'That was a hell of a lot of money,' remarks Chinaglia. Soon after, Wilson joined him. 'A scout called Vittorio Galli spotted us,' recalls Wilson. 'He was once a forward with Lazio. He told the club Internapoli had these two good players coming through and ought to watch out for them. I was supposed to go to Napoli but Lazio offered me more money. Internapoli were willing to release me from the agreement with Napoli.'

The departure of the two players signalled the beginning of the end of the Neapolitan club. Relegated to *Serie D* in 1971, the club closed in 1973. 'Once Chinaglia and Wilson left, Internapoli disintegrated,' adds Di Marzio. 'It was like a balloon that blew and blew and then burst.'

Piero Caramella remembers Chinaglia returning home to Cardiff, shortly after he signed for Lazio, to visit his family. 'He told me, "I wish I had been bought by Cagliari. They have Luigi Riva so I wouldn't have had to worry about scoring goals." Riva was Italy's finest marksman at the time and that year he had topped the goalscoring charts for a second time. 'Giorgio was worried about having the responsibility to score all the goals.'

While staying in South Wales during the summer he joined Lazio, Chinaglia maintained his fitness by training at his old stomping ground, Sophia Gardens. 'We played against each other, just me and him,' says Caramella. 'He had his goal, I had mine. We must have trained for about two hours and I was shattered. Then this team of boys came along and Giorgio said, "Can we join you?" I said I'd be a goalkeeper because I was so tired but Giorgio carried on playing and scored I don't know how many goals. It was like he had just started. In fact, there was a scout there watching and he came over to Giorgio and talked to him for about half an hour.'

Andrea Delnero, who was at the park as well, also recalls that day. 'When we finished this scout came up to us and said to me, "I see you've got some star." He wanted to take Giorgio to Cardiff City and Giorgio started laughing. "I've been, they didn't want to know!" I told this chap, "He's playing in Italy now, for Lazio."'

Alan Wilkins saw his old housemate after he had joined the *Serie A* club. Chinaglia visited him in Newport since Wilkins was still playing for Lovell's Athletic. Lazio's new signing, who by now was a member of the Italian Under-21 squad, was wearing a smart all-blue tracksuit with ITALIA emblazoned across the chest. 'He had lost so much weight in the Army that when Lazio signed him they sent him up to the mountains to eat steak, pasta and chop trees so he could get his weight back,' says Wilkins. 'I asked him if he wanted to go up to the Rhondda and see my mum and dad but he said he'd already been to see them. I was very impressed with that. That showed what a good lad he was.'

During the exceptionally hot summer of 1969 the Romans had got their man but Lazio were not the first club on the scene. As Chinaglia recalls, 'Internapoli promised me to Fiorentina but I didn't accept that. Then they had a bigger offer from Cagliari, a bigger offer from Inter and a bigger offer from Milan. But the biggest offer came from Lazio. Lazio paid them six months ahead of time. I didn't play the last few months of the *Serie C* championship because they were afraid of me getting hurt.' Chinaglia believes his absence cost Internapoli promotion. 'We finished third. We could have won the championship but I couldn't play, and I was top goalscorer with 14 goals. In the last eight games we won just two and lost four or five. I don't think Internapoli wanted to go up. There was a lot of politics.'

In 1969 Lazio was very much Rome's second club, just as Internapoli had been second in Naples. The one championship brought to the capital, in 1942, had been won by Roma. Lazio, known as i *biancocelesti* – the sky blues – yo-yoed between the first and second divisions while Roma were an established *Serie A* club, like Juventus, Milan and Inter, and had also won the Fairs Cup, the forerunner of the UEFA Cup, in 1961. Lazio's solitary honour was the Coppa Italia, the country's domestic cup competition, in 1958.

But the club had just won promotion from *Serie B* and optimism was high. In the sumptuous surrounds of Villa Miani, a manor in the elegant Monte Mario area of the city, Lazio's players and officials sipped champagne to celebrate their success. Umberto Lenzini gave a speech and mentioned four promising young players who were about to join 'the Lazio family' – Chinaglia, Wilson, midfielder Franco Nanni and goalkeeper Michelangelo Sulfaro. Three of them – Chinaglia; Wilson and Nanni – would be ever-present in the championship-winning team five years later but Sulfaro would leave Lazio for Fiorentina in

1971. Omar Sivori was convinced Lazio had erred in buying Chinaglia. He went as far as to say, 'Chinaglia will never play in *Serie A*. He expresses the elegance of an elephant who has been ordered to move in a china shop.'

The plump, fearsome-looking coach, Juan Carlos Lorenzo, was in his second spell as Lazio's coach when Chinaglia arrived from Naples. He was first hired in 1962 but left two years later to coach, of all teams, Roma, their bitter rivals. *Traditore!* – traitor! – cried the Lazio *tifosi*. He returned in 1968, won promotion at the first attempt and all was forgiven. Lorenzo was so concerned by Sivori's scathing opinion of Chinaglia that he persuaded Lenzini to sign another striker, Vicenza's Mario Tomy, as cover should the former Internapoli player fail to adapt to *Serie A*.

Lorenzo had played centre-forward in four different countries, for Boca Juniors in his native Argentina, for Sampdoria and Genoa in Italy, Nancy in France and Rayo Vallecano in Spain. As a manager, he had a reputation for being a tough man who produced tough teams. He was in charge of a cynical and violent Argentinian side during the 1966 World Cup, a side England manager Alf Ramsey described as 'animals'. Two years earlier he had been banned by the *Federcalcio* for six months after running onto the pitch during a Lazio–Torino match and ordering his players to kick the opposition – 'encouraging rough play and making menacing gestures' was the exact charge – and on another occasion Lorenzo, incensed by his team's defeat, burned the shirts and boots of his players.

But he was far from being a one-dimensional character. Lorenzo was highly superstitious. In every hotel he stayed he insisted on sleeping in room number seven. If, *en route* to the stadium, he saw a black cat from the window of the coach he would order the driver to change route. He was also studious about the game, almost to the point of obsession. In his study he kept files on African wingers and Korean forwards.

Lorenzo instantly struck a rapport with Chinaglia. He became the player's first real mentor, teaching him how to shield the ball with his body, how to evade man-to-man markers inside the penalty area, improving his shooting and increasing his acceleration from a standing position. 'Lorenzo was good. A bit crazy, but he was good,' recalls Chinaglia. 'He taught me a lot of things – not to be afraid, to do what I wanted to do on the field, not to worry about anything. Even though I was one of the younger players, he said I was a leader. He was a hard man but not with me. He knew his cake, and the cake he left alone.'

Giancarlo Oddi was in his third year at Lazio when Chinaglia arrived. 'Lorenzo was a very important man in Giorgio's formation,' explains the former defender. 'At the start, when he first came to Lazio, he had some rough edges and his attitude wasn't quite right. Lorenzo tried to sharpen him up. In the beginning Giorgio retaliated but in the end he realised he was trying to teach him, to train him. He realised listening to Lorenzo would be beneficial so he followed him.'

The Argentinian's influence could be seen during Chinaglia's full *Serie A* début, against Milan in Rome on 28 September 1969. It was the third week of the season. Lorenzo preferred the more experienced Gian Piero Ghio in the first two matches, a 1–1 draw against Torino and a 1–0 defeat in Bologna. Chinaglia made his first *Serie A* appearance against Bologna as a second-half substitute and made an impression. 'When I came on we were losing 1–0 and we still lost 1–0 but I won eight corner-kicks in ten minutes all by myself,' recalls Chinaglia.

Against Milan, crowned champions of Europe four months earlier and inspired by the graceful playmaker Gianni Rivera, Chinaglia was picked from the start. In front of a capacity 80,000 crowd he had a torrid first half as the Milan defence, marshalled by Italian international stopper Roberto Rosato, anticipated his every move. At the interval he returned to the dressing-room a demoralised heap. But there Lorenzo re-motivated him. He took him aside, said *'Giuoca come sai'* – just play your game – and patted him on the back. He was a different player in the second half and five minutes from the end he scored a sensational winner. Giuseppe Wilson hit a long ball towards the corner flag to the right of the Milan goal. Chinaglia chased it, controlled it, dribbled past Angelo Anquilletti, the Italian international right-back before curving the ball around the advancing Fabio

Cudicini. 'People went nuts,' recalls Chinaglia. 'The next home game was Fiorentina. They were the reigning league champions. We were losing 1–0 and we won 5–1. I scored two goals. That game was unbelievable.'

Wilson, too, was playing in the first team. The leap from *Serie C* to *Serie A* had been smooth for both men. 'Once we arrived at Lazio,' says Wilson, 'we made an impact and Lorenzo played us straight away. I had a lovely rapport with Lorenzo. He was very complimentary to me and Giorgio. He said that for Lazio we were a luxury.' After just a couple of months in the capital, the Lazio *tifosi* had adopted Chinaglia as their *bandiera* – flagship player.

'I had done National Service with Giorgio and played with him in the military team,' says Giancarlo Oddi. 'I had no doubts he would make it. Although he was playing in *Serie C* at the time, he was of *Serie A* calibre. My thoughts were proved right.'

Midfielder Franco Nanni had also encountered Chinaglia before they both moved to Rome. 'I played against him in *Serie C*. I was playing for Trapani when he was at Internapoli. I had heard about this big, powerful man, this machine, so I was curious to see him. In the beginning at Lazio he didn't do too well. He was quite rough and raw and he was impetuous. But Lorenzo looked after him and he was soon noticed. Lorenzo wanted him because there were not many forceful forwards around at the time. Giorgio was his ram.'

At the beginning of November, Lorenzo's men were seen as title contenders. Much to everyone's surprise they were lying fourth in *Serie A* while Chinaglia was earning comparisons with Silvio Piola, the great centre-forward who played for the club from 1934–43 and who starred in Italy's World Cup triumph of 1938. Piola was one of his growing army of admirers: 'Looking at Chinaglia I find myself in him. I see myself in him.' Another was the former Inter coach Helenio Herrera, now in charge of Roma: 'Chinaglia belongs to a species of footballer which is in extinction.'

Reality soon set in at the Olimpico as Lazio slid down the table. But they finished the season strongly, beating both Inter and Juventus in

Rome to clinch a respectable ninth place. 'We were very good at home but terrible away,' says Chinaglia who ended the season with 14 goals, an excellent total during the days of *catenaccio*. That season 'Long John' – his nickname at the club – was re-acquainted with English football courtesy of the Anglo-Italian Cup, a bad-tempered competition which, unsuccessfully, tried to marry the physical English style with the cynical Italian game.

Lazio were drawn with Sunderland and Wolves. For Chinaglia the match against Wolves at Molineux was a day to forget. He was sent off for the first time in his career. 'I went to see him before that game,' says Gordon Roberts. 'I asked him how he was doing in Italy. He said, "There's only one player who has scored more than me (he was referring to Luigi Riva) and most of his goals are penalties." That was typical Giorgio!' On a miserable Saturday afternoon in the West Midlands, Lazio lost 1–0, Mike Bailey firing the winner midway through the second half. Lazio thought they had levelled in the dying minutes, the players claiming goalkeeper Phil Parkes had dropped the ball over the line. The entire team surrounded Italian referee Ettore Carminati who said no goal, and when the others backed off, Chinaglia carried on protesting. Carminati lost patience and pointed Chinaglia to the tunnel. Asked about English football after the game he revealed his bitterness towards it. 'It simply isn't football,' he said. 'You aren't allowed to play the game.'

His exploits in *Serie A* had not escaped the attention of Ferruccio Valcareggi, the craggy-faced coach of the Italian national side. For the World Cup that year, in Mexico, Chinaglia made the shortlist of 40 players but he did not make the final 22-man squad. Still, Valcareggi took Chinaglia to Mexico for the experience. Recalls Salvatore Amodeo, 'Giorgio was one of two or three youngsters that were taken unofficially.' Amodeo travelled to Mexico to follow Italy's fortunes and met with his old school friend in Mexico City. 'They were staying in a beautiful villa, the Parques des Princes, just outside Mexico City. Valcareggi wanted Giorgio to mix with players like Luigi Riva and Gianni Rivera. Giorgio took me into the hotel and I saw all the players. It was more exciting for me! In fairness to Giorgio, he hadn't changed. He was the same bloke he was in Cardiff. He wasn't the airs-and-graces type.'

Earmarked as a future Italian international, Chinaglia returned from Mexico one of Serie A's most exciting prospects. He and Connie lived in a beautiful apartment in Via Baldo degli Ubaldi, near the Vatican, and started investing in property, buying apartments throughout the city. Before the 1970–71 season started the 23-year-old told journalists of his vision for the club. 'I am determined to take Lazio to the highest peak. I want to contribute to the transformation. I will stay here until we become important, until we are envied by Roma, until we are admired wherever we go. Lazio is not simply a club, it's a faith, like a sickness.'

But Chinaglia's second year was a disaster. Lazio won only five games out of 30 and were relegated. Inevitably, 'Don Juan' Lorenzo was sacked. Chinaglia's pre-season fear that 'one player can't change the face of the team. Lazio is still fragile, made up of too many lightweights' was realised. The vile winter Italy experienced in 1971 affected the Romans more than any other team. Despite Chinaglia's presence, Lazio were the smallest side in *Serie A*. In the mud and snow, their most influential midfielders, Giuseppe Massa and Ferruccio Mazzola, sank without trace.

As for Chinaglia, he had an appalling nine months scoring only seven goals. Franco Nanni defends the forward's contribution that season: 'Giorgio still did his bit. We had the cannon but we couldn't provide the cannon with the ammunition.' The press and *tifosi* were not so understanding. The same people who fêted the striker in 1969–70 now turned on him. The media blamed his married life for his torrid form. 'Giorgio is no longer Giorgio,' wrote one journalist. 'He has discovered the pleasure of intimate love.' Outside his apartment in the heart of the city, supporters shouted obscenities and relentlessly sounded their car horns. His wife, too, was insulted and ridiculed every time she ventured outside. During this turbulent period, Connie was expecting their first child, Cynthia, and as a precaution Chinaglia moved her to Naples to live with her parents, so unbearable was life in Rome.

The newly-weds nearly always ran into trouble if they went into the city to eat or visit a nightclub. Piero Caramella visited his old friend in Rome at the height of this hate campaign. 'He was nervous, really nervous. He was getting a lot of stick from fans and reporters. We went to a restaurant to eat – me, my wife, Giorgio and his wife. As we left, he was walking out with my wife and I was with his wife. There were photographers and reporters outside and he was afraid they would make out he was having an affair. Giorgio and Connie said they had better walk out together otherwise the reporters would write things which were not true.'

Later that night the Chinaglias and Caramellas went to a nightclub, Jackie O's on Via Bon Compagni. Jackie O's was one of Rome's smartest clubs and a favourite haunt of the Chinaglias, but even here they encountered problems. 'The wives had been to the ladies' room and were coming back to our table,' says Caramella. 'There was this man in the way and he wouldn't move for them. Giorgio threw a table mat at him first, then he got up and punched him. I went over and calmed him down. They threw the other guy out. They knew Giorgio at the club and treated him like a personality. We could have stayed but we left after that.'

The Fairs Cup, later renamed the UEFA Cup, offered Lazio and Chinaglia a welcome diversion from the turbulence of *Serie A*. It was the first time Lazio had qualified for one of Europe's three competitions. They also had a tantalising first-round draw, against holders Arsenal. The tie threw up an extraordinary head-to-head: Chinaglia versus his former Swansea colleague John Roberts. Both had come a long way since their apprentice days sweeping stands at the Vetch, hoping to find loose change under the seats. 'It was a strange feeling because I'd not seen Giorgio since he left Swansea,' recalls Roberts, who had signed for Arsenal in 1968 and had been converted from forward to centre-half. Arsenal's management team of Bertie Mee and Don Howe had identified Chinaglia as Lazio's main threat. Roberts was given the task of marking Chinaglia in both legs.

The first match, in Rome, was a violent, bad-tempered affair. Arsenal went 2–0 up early in the second-half, John Radford scoring twice in four minutes. 'Then they started the silly stuff,' says Roberts. 'I remember turning round and seeing our defender, Sammy Nelson, flat out on the ground. Someone had punched him. Some of the Italian players were punching and spitting.' Bob Wilson revealed one Lazio player stepped on his boot and spat at his face.

Arsenal held on to their two-goal lead until the last few minutes. 'We were coasting and it looked all over. Then Giorgio Chinaglia came good,' adds Don Howe, then Arsenal's coach. He struck twice in the last five minutes. His first was a low drive past Wilson, the second from the penalty spot after Frank McClintock was ruled to have handled the ball. Chinaglia had salvaged a 2–2 draw for his team.

'He had matured enormously. He was stronger, more dedicated,' says Roberts. 'He'd lost weight as well. Maybe he benefited from the Italian coaching. They were far more advanced in things like diet and training. It obviously turned him into a better player. He was difficult to mark. He could hold the ball up and get into the box.'

As the Arsenal players left the Olimpico the Italian supporters threw oranges and missiles at them, and there were scuffles involving both sets of players inside the tunnel. The real trouble started after the game, at the L'Augustea restaurant where the players went for a post-match banquet organised by Lazio. Because of events which occurred on the field, the atmosphere inside the restaurant was tense. Recalls Don Howe, 'Some niggly things went on during the game, like pushing and shoving.' So the players settled their scores in the street outside. The fight started after several Lazio players attacked Ray Kennedy, Arsenal's striker, as he left the restaurant. Within seconds it had erupted into a street brawl involving most of the players. Some onlookers claimed Juan Carlos Lorenzo was encouraging his men to attack their English counterparts. Chinaglia, though, did not get involved. 'Giorgio and I were chatting away,' recounts Roberts, 'when all of a sudden there was this commotion outside. We both went out and there were all these players fighting in the street. We tried to calm it down and Bertie Mee was practically carrying his players back onto the bus.'

Ray Kennedy later recalled the fight started when the Arsenal players ridiculed the leather purses presented to them by Lazio officials and started throwing them around. They may have been fashionable in Italy but in Britain they were considered an effeminate accessory. 'Looking back, those leather purses were lovely,' says Roberts. 'In those days British men wouldn't have carried them around but now they would.'

Arsenal easily won the return a fortnight later. Lazio threatened to boycott the game but UEFA, unimpressed, insisted they play. John Radford and George Armstrong scored in the Gunners' 2–0 victory. 'They got a terrible reception from the Arsenal crowd when they went out for their warm-up,' recalls John Roberts. 'You could see the Lazio players didn't want to be at Highbury.' This time there were no heroics from Chinaglia as Arsenal ran out comfortable winners. 'Giorgio was very quiet at Highbury,' adds Roberts. 'All Lazio's players were like mice. They didn't want to know. Bertie Mee said "Let them go out first so they're on their own" and you could hear the booing inside our dressing-room.' Lazio's first European adventure lasted a mere 180 minutes. They had done themselves little credit on or off the pitch and UEFA hit them with a two-year ban from European competition for the scenes in Rome.

'It was very calm at Highbury. I got the impression they wanted to get this match out of the way,' remarks Don Howe. 'We took the game to them. We had a feeling morale was not too high with Lazio. In those days they were the underdogs of Rome. One year they were up, the next year they were down. They were one of *Serie A*'s bottom-four teams. They weren't the force they became at the end of the 1990s, nowhere near. They couldn't match Juventus or Milan. They were looked upon as a very ordinary Italian team.'

CHAPTER EIGHT

DURING THE SUMMER of 1971 Umberto Lenzini scoured Italy for a man to replace 'Don Juan' Lorenzo. He finally chose the affable Tommaso Maestrelli, a native of Pisa and once a methodical right-half with Bari, Roma and Lucchese. He made one appearance for his country against Denmark in 1948. Italy lost 5–3 and Maestrelli never played for the national team again.

The choice of Maestrelli surprised Chinaglia and his team-mates. Maestrelli had coached Foggia the previous season and Foggia, like Lazio, had been relegated to Serie B. Naturally, they felt Lorenzo had suffered a raw deal but Maestrelli's record impressed Lenzini. Lazio did not have the financial clout of the northern clubs and the Tuscan appeared to relish working on a limited budget. He had taken Reggina from Serie C to Serie B, and Foggia from Serie B to Serie A.

When his appointment was publicly announced, Maestrelli, who was known for his extravagant head of greying hair, made a peaceable pronouncement: 'I will speak little and that little will be seen to be a lot. This is a profession which is not a profession. We will love one another and avoid any misunderstanding. I consider loyalty the best gift given on this planet. We will grow together.'

For the first week of pre-season there was a barrier between Maestrelli and Chinaglia. The striker was still upset about Lorenzo's dismissal but that barrier soon disintegrated as the softly spoken Maestrelli demonstrated his man-management skills. 'Maestrelli was the man we needed. He was excellent, perfect,' recalls Chinaglia. 'He used to work on feelings, the mental aspect. We used to have arguments. "Why do you spend so much time with players who don't play?" I'd ask. He'd say, "Because if you get injured I have to make sure they are ready to come in. You first-team people know what to do." He was the best manager I worked with.'

Chinaglia could have stayed in *Serie A*. Despite a lacklustre 1970–71 four clubs wanted to buy him – Juventus, Milan, Inter and Napoli. Despite the offers, Chinaglia decided to remain in Rome. 'I wanted to stay, come back to the first division and then see what to do,' he says. 'I had a debt to Lazio. The only way they could come back, no offence, is if I was with them. They tripled my salary so I was being paid the same as a first-division footballer, if not more.'

Before the *Serie B* championship started Maestrelli had already brought one trophy to the Olimpico, albeit the meaningless Alps Cup, a competition open to four Swiss clubs and four Italian. Here, in Basle, the first signs emerged of a special relationship between the coach and player. Chinaglia, suffering with tonsillitis, looked certain to miss the first game, against Lugano. Maestrelli came up with a homespun remedy, a lemon. He squeezed the juice into a glass and told the bemused Chinaglia to drink it. Chinaglia claimed the vitamin C gave him renewed strength and he hit a hat-trick in the 4–1 win. In this competition he scored ten goals including two in the final against Basle which Lazio won 3–1. The tournament had restored the confidence he had lost the previous season.

Of course, the real objective was a return to *Serie A*. Maestrelli promised the *tifosi* he would win promotion at the first attempt and this he did with more or less the same players he inherited. There had been one important signing, Luigi Martini from Livorno, a midfielder Maestrelli later converted into a fine defender. (The balding Martini was to be involved in a famous dressing-room bust-up with Chinaglia after a UEFA Cup game in Switzerland.) Lazio finished second behind

Ternana, thanks almost entirely to Chinaglia's goals. He scored a remarkable 21 goals in 34 matches that season. He was rewarded with more than promotion. He became the first-ever *Serie B* footballer to play for the national team, Ferruccio Valcareggi using him as a substitute in Bulgaria.

Aside from 'Long John', meant affectionately, his other nickname, used derisively by notherners and also Roma supporters, was *Il Gobo* – the hunchback – because of his stooped posture.

After the promotion, Milan were prepared to offer Lazio a world record £800,000 for Chinaglia – almost double the current record, the £400,000 Juventus paid Varese for striker Pietro Anastasi. 'I'm not surprised to hear that he's worth £800,000,' said John Irvine, who had left Swansea to scout for Carlisle United. 'He had great ability, even at 15. He had this great flair for getting goals. I remember well a West Wales Cup match against Milford Athletic which we won 7–2 and Giorgio scored six. I always remember their centre-half saying after the game: "If that's what macaroni does for you, get me some quick."' But Lazio, fearing a boycott of season ticket sales, refused to sell. Mario Chinaglia, described it thus: 'There would have been riots in the streets of Rome if they had dared to sell him.'

In the summer of 1972 Maestrelli began to build the Lazio that would, in two years time, win the championship. 'I told Maestrelli not to buy old players,' says Chinaglia. 'We had some old players when we got out of *Serie B*, then we got rid of them. Now we were in *Serie A* we had to get young players.' Maestrelli made six new signings – goalkeeper Felice Pulici from Novara, stopper Sergio Petrelli from Roma, playmaker Mario Frustalupi from Inter and the skilled midfielder Luciano Re Cecconi from Foggia. Maestrelli had coached the blond Re Cecconi at Foggia. When he left for Lazio he told him, 'I'll see you in Rome.'

Although Chinaglia had topped the shopping lists of the big clubs, he had pledged his future to Maestrelli. He had made his peace with the city, or rather the city had made its peace with him. He opened a menswear shop, which Connie ran, and out at the Esposizione Universale di Roma, otherwise known simply as EUR, a district in the south of Rome opened by Mussolini in the 1920s, he built a tennis club with six courts. He had also learned from the traumatic experiences of 1970–71. The Chinaglias now lived on the outskirts of the city, on Via Aurelia, where they would be a less accessible target for any irate *tifosi*.

Little was expected of Lazio in the 1972–73 season. According to the pundits, like all clubs that come up from *Serie B*, they would do well to achieve *salvezza*, to avoid relegation. But the club had other ideas. Maestrelli's side were a revelation and on the very last Sunday of the season they were involved in a gripping three-club battle for the championship with Milan and Juventus. 'Football-wise the 1973 team was better than the one that won the championship a year later,' reveals Chinaglia. 'We played a bit like Holland's national team. People said we copied them. We didn't. It came by luck. Things worked out that way. We played much better the year we didn't win it than the year we did. Everybody loved the way we played.'

Maestrelli might have found himself out of work during the first month of the season. Lazio had finished last in their Coppa Italia group, beaten by Brindisi, Taranto and Napoli. The *tifosi*, possibly more fickle in Rome than anywhere else in the world, were demanding his head, as Franco Nanni recalls. 'We had a bad start in the friendlies and the Coppa Italia. The fans were not happy and there was talk Maestrelli was about to be sacked. We were not playing well and we were losing. Our first three *Serie A* games were heavy games, against Inter, Fiorentina and Juventus. Maestrelli's fate was going to be decided on the results of those games.'

The players saved their coach by starting well, drawing with Inter, beating Fiorentina and drawing with Juventus. Maestrelli strengthened his defence by making two crucial switches. Luigi Martini was moved from midfield to right-back and Giancarlo Oddi was moved from right-back to play alongside Giuseppe Wilson in the heart of defence. To everyone's surprise Lazio took over the leadership of *Serie A* by winning the next four games. Their midfield was much admired. Re Cecconi, athletic and inventive, was dubbed 'Cecconetzer' because of his likeness – physical as well – to West Germany's Gunter Netzer. Mario Frustalupi was the artist, dictating the play and controlling the tempo of most matches. Sergio Garlachelli, quick and brilliant at close-range passing inside the penalty area, was an ideal foil for Chinaglia. In an era of defensive football, when *catenaccio* was the rage, the Romans stood out with a more adventurous style.

Lazio had set the pace but they slackened in the winter months and fell to fourth behind Milan, Juventus and Inter. They picked up again in the spring when they rejoined the title race with nine consecutive victories. They included wins over Roma and leaders Milan. In the latter Chinaglia scored the winner in the 2–1 home win, a 30-yard thunderbolt that broke two fingers of Pierangelo Belli, Milan's stand-in goalkeeper, who tried to tip the ball to safety.

An incident before the second Rome derby of the season exposed the infantile, self-destructive face of Roman football and offered an explanation as to why the championship had not been won by one of the city's clubs for more than thirty years.

At Lazio's matches Maestrelli was always accompanied by his two young sons, twins Massimo and Maurizio. 'They are my lucky mascots,' the coach once explained. Before the game with Roma, Umberto Lenzini found them playing outside the dressing-rooms and ordered them to leave. When Maestrelli emerged from the dressing-room just minutes before the kick-off he discovered they had disappeared. Lenzini told him they had been sent away. 'By whom?' Maestrelli asked angrily. 'By me!' shouted the president. 'And if you don't look out, you'll go too!' Maestrelli, who had yet to agree a contract for 1973–74, went to look for the twins, saying he did not care if he left Lazio. Despite the abbreviated team-talk, Lazio won 2–0. The victory soothed tempers and the following week both president and coach had made up. After the row, Chinaglia laconically summed up life at Lazio: 'The rows tend to take place during the week while the matches are still won on the Sunday.' What would have happened had Lazio lost the derby is anybody's guess.

Lazio may have been enjoying success on the field but personally

Chinaglia endured a difficult period after Christmas 1973. He had not scored for weeks, had lost his place in the national team and, clearly agitated, blamed his team-mates for the slump, claiming they were not passing the ball to him. Some years later Luigi Martini remarked on Chinaglia's behaviour towards his team-mates: 'He had a terrible habit of being up and down. One day he was miserable, the next he was happy. He used to admire himself in front of a mirror as if he was a monument. On the field he wanted all of us to be his servants and this I could never take. He was quarrelsome, he would fight with photographers and think we were all his subjects. The thing was, outside football he was a delightful and pleasant man.'

In the halls of the Hotel Americana, the *ritiro* hotel 15 kilometres outside Rome where the Lazio players stayed the three days before a match, Chinaglia was often seen walking with Maestrelli, his arm around him, telling him his thoughts on the team and what could be done to make him score more goals. 'Tommaso, it's useless to play Martini and Re Cecconi because if someone from the youth team plays he will give me the ball straight away, I shoot and score goals,' he would say. Maestrelli knew how to placate him. He listened, made him feel his views were valued but never implemented his suggestions. '*Si, buono Giorgio*' – yes, good Giorgio – he would gently tell the forward, knowing that he would walk away and soon forget about the conversation. 'Maestrelli was very intelligent, a man of great sensitivity,' explains Luigi Martini. 'He understood what Chinaglia needed and made him believe he was doing what he wanted him to do. In the heat of the moment you couldn't reason with Giorgio. When he was huffing and puffing Maestrelli would cave in to him. When Giorgio had calmed down he would make him believe that his own way was right.'

Whenever Chinaglia scored he would run to the Lazio bench to embrace Maestrelli. After training Chinaglia often visited his house, in the Collina Fleming area of the city, to discuss football. The coach listened but that is all. 'You could ask Maestrelli about going to the bar, the pub, the nightclub,' says Giuseppe Wilson, 'but there was one thing you couldn't ask him about – the team. When it came to naming the team he was the only one who could do it and no one else.'

Chinaglia was Maestrelli's *figlio prediletto* – the favourite son – yet he was careful not to isolate the other players and make them feel inferior. 'They were like father and son,' recalls Vincenzo D'Amico, the young midfielder who would make such a huge impact in the championship season. 'Giorgio loved Maestrelli and for Maestrelli, Giorgio was like a son.' But D'Amico confirms the 25-year-old Chinaglia had no say in team affairs despite his close relationship with the coach. 'Maestrelli was too intelligent to be influenced by him. He made him believe he had an influence but he always did things his way. Giorgio wasn't the only one close to Maestrelli. All the players had a good relationship with him. Giorgio maybe felt he was special but no one else got that impression.'

The coach's skilful and patient handling of Chinaglia could be seen during the team's training sessions at Tor di Quinto. The team's eight-a-side *partitelle* – practice matches – were fiercely contested. The players took them seriously and no one more so than Chinaglia. Aware his mood was intrinsically related to scoring goals, Maestrelli would do his utmost to end a game after he had scored the winning goal. Life with Chinaglia could be difficult if he was not scoring.

Former goalkeeper Felice Pulici recalls the striker's strong personality: 'He was someone who wanted to play all the time and score constantly. He was a very egotistical player. He wanted the ball all the time. He thought on the field he was the only thing that mattered.'

The goals dried up for 'Long John' halfway through the 1972–73 season and the team's title challenge began to falter. As a result, Chinaglia became agitated and nervous on the field. Walter Colli, a writer for the Rome-based daily newspaper, *Corriere dello Sport*, watched him in a home match against modest Atalanta during this barren spell. With Lazio losing 1–0, Chinaglia's personal crisis deepened as Atalanta's goalkeeper, Marcello Grassi, denied him at every turn. Chinaglia, wrote Colli, 'was caged worse than a tiger . . . he shot and was angry like a madman because Grassi was saving everything. For poor Giorgio it was another dry Sunday.' Much to Chinaglia's chagrin, Re Cecconi stole the headlines the next day after firing the winner in the 2–1 win. 'RE CECCONI HA CONQUISTATO L'OLIMPICO' – Re Cecconi conquered the Olimpico – said *Corriere*. Another player had stolen his thunder, something Chinaglia never liked.

Chinaglia brooded whenever he failed to score, the most famous example coming during Lazio's championship-winning season, after a home game against Milan in December 1973. Lazio won thanks to a last-minute goal from Re Cecconi. After the game the players boarded the bus that would take them back to the Hotel Americana. Chinaglia was furious he had not scored and Re Cecconi had again been the hero. As he took his seat he shouted at the midfielder, 'You did not give me one decent ball! Not one decent ball!' Striker Renzo Garlaschelli tried to calm him down. He put his arm over his shoulder and said, 'Come on, Giorgio, we've won the game!' It made no difference. Chinaglia ignored Garlaschelli, sat down and just stared out of the window. Maestrelli noticed the outburst and shook his head in disbelief.

'Away from the pitch he was a real joy, but on the pitch he was unbearable,' says Franco Nanni. 'And if the newspapers said anything bad about him he would go mad.' He would not have enjoyed a spiteful article by Giovanni Arpino in the daily newspaper, *La Stampa*, written during the lean period in 1972–73: 'If King Kong Chinaglia prefers an amorous sortie to a dribbling run he passes out of our sphere of interest.' The press were once again pointing the finger at his private life, that his form was suffering because he and Connie were more interested in *la dolce vita*.

With less than three months of the season left Lazio were outside the top three. Chinaglia was struggling to find the net and to make things worse he had been excluded from Italy's last match, a World Cup qualifier against Turkey in Istanbul. Chinaglia was, as the Italians say, *in crisi* – in crisis. If Lazio were to challenge for the *Serie A* championship, they needed their star forward to rediscover his early-season form. Armando Taddel, the Lazio physio, approached Maestrelli with a possible solution.

'Do you believe in the curse?' asked Taddel.

'Yes, why? Who has got it?' replied the coach.

'Maybe Chinaglia. My mother knows how to get rid of the curse.'

'OK. Organise it.'

In a move which makes former England coach Glenn Hoddle's predilection for spiritual healing look tame, Maestrelli agreed to an attempt at removing the 'curse' – a way of saying they believed Chinaglia to be jinxed. Maestrelli's compliance surprised many. As a devout Roman Catholic, he could well have regarded such antics as witchcraft. The session would take place at the home of Taddel's friend, Giulio Scio, a warehouse worker and attendant at the club's training ground in Tor di Quinto.

Maestrelli had only to convince his forward to take part. 'Go, go. Give it a try,' he said to Chinaglia, who reluctantly agreed. Taddel was told to pick up his 71-year-old mother, Gina, and bring her to Scio's house. There they sat around a table in the kitchen and Taddel's mother put her thumb in a plate of oil and water. She rubbed her thumb across Chinaglia's forehead three times. Each time she said, 'In the name of Jesus, Joseph and Mary, if you have the curse make it go away.'

Taddel had every reason to feel pleased with himself. The following Sunday, against Napoli in the Olimpico, Chinaglia ended his drought in a convincing 3–0 win, scoring from what seemed an off-side position four minutes from the end.

With Lazio in the limelight Chinaglia had become a marked man, a cynosure. No game illustrated this better than the match with Napoli. Afterwards Chinaglia claimed two of their defenders tried to intimidate him. He accused Giovanni Vavassori, Napoli's stopper, of spitting at him after he scored his goal, and Angelo Rimbano, their full-back, of threatening to break his leg. Vavassori denied the allegation. Rimbano, on the other hand, fervently admitted it. 'Sometimes,' complained Chinaglia, 'I'm kicked and spat at before I go onto the field. I've always got three men that mark me. I enjoy it when I play at home. When I play away, they don't let me play at all.'

Lazio hit another purple patch in the final weeks of the 1972–73 campaign but they were denied a crucial victory against Inter in the San Siro when Inter's international striker Roberto Boninsegna equalised with a blatant handball. On the last day of the season three teams could win the championship – Milan, Juventus and Lazio. Milan were top with 44 points, Juventus and Lazio shared second with 43. All three had away matches: Milan were at Verona, Juventus, ominously, were at Roma and Lazio were at Napoli.

If they were to be crowned champions, Lazio needed to win and hope the other two slipped up. It was an unlikely scenario. Verona were in the bottom half of the table and would Roma really help Lazio win the title? At half-time it looked possible. Lazio were drawing 0–0 while both Milan and Juventus were losing, 3–1 and 1–0 respectively. Chinaglia and his colleagues had one hand on *Lo Scudetto*. The championship was decided in the final six minutes. Milan lost 5–3 in Verona but Juventus turned the tables in Rome winning 2–1, Antonello Cuccureddu scoring the winner three minutes from time, while Lazio went down 1–0 in Naples, Giuseppe Damiani scoring in the 84th minute.

When the final whistle blew, Chinaglia, angry at the result and the fact he had failed to score, threw the ball into the stands. Had Lazio won in Naples they would have played Juventus in a *spareggio scudetto* – a play-off to decide the championship – since they would have been level on points. Goal difference did not count.

'We had just come up from the second division,' recalls Chinaglia. 'We did more than we should have done. We knew we would win the following year. We knew the competition out there was not as good as us.' Inevitably, there were cries from Lazio that Roma had deliberately lost to Juventus to stop them winning the title. Helenio Herrera, Roma's coach, was accused of fielding 'a couple of soft players' but Felice Pulici says Lazio had only themselves to blame. 'We lost it because we didn't have the maturity to win it. At the end of the first half we knew Milan and Juventus were losing. We were drawing but we didn't have the strength or maturity to kill the game off. At the end of the day your adversaries can make all the plots they want but there is nothing to stop you going out and winning the game yourself.'

A philosophical Giuseppe Wilson agrees. 'You can say the championship was stolen from us but you can also say we gave it away. That's the way it went. It happened. There's nothing you can do. We could have won it but we didn't.'

According to Franco Nanni, the title had really been lost a few weeks earlier, in the match against Inter when Boninsegna's handball robbed them of a point. 'Everyone saw it except the referee. That was the relevant game, not the one in Naples. It was disappointing we didn't win in 1973. We should have won it. A lot of things have been said about the Roma–Juventus game but I have my doubts about them.'

Luigi Martini also believes Roma played honestly. 'I don't think they threw the game. Juventus's winning goal was a fortuitous shot. I believe in the purity of sport, I don't believe in bad faith.'

Lazio's ultimate downfall was a poor goalscoring record rather than any machinations on the final Sunday. Because of Maestrelli's tactical system, which required Chinaglia to drop back into midfield to bring Renzo Garlaschelli and Luciano Re Cecconi into the action, the forward scored a disappointing 10 league goals. 'If Giorgio had scored a few more goals we would have won the title,' says Giancarlo Oddi. 'When we did win it the following year he more than doubled his total and was fundamental to the success. But not every year can be the same.'

The Romans scored an unspectacular 33 goals all season, half the number Milan scored and 12 less than Juventus. A reason for this modest goal tally, explains Felice Pulici, was Chinaglia's honesty during matches, a trait he picked up during his formative years as an apprentice in English football. 'He never took advantage of situations. If he was challenged irregularly in the penalty area he wouldn't take advantage. He could have made meals out of small things but he didn't. He was a little bit naïve that way and it was because he wanted to play so much.'

For the next season Maestrelli adjusted the playing system. Franco Nanni was given more of a holding role in midfield, allowing Chinaglia to play more as a traditional forward. 'It was the same team but tactically we changed,' explained the striker. 'In 1973 we played like the Dutch side, the second year we put one midfielder back and that gave me and Garlaschelli more space.' Lazio began the season with a 3–0 win over Lanerossi Vicenza in Rome, Chinaglia opening the scoring in the seventh minute. That was followed by a 1–0 win over Sampdoria. Then came a sticky patch, losing at Juventus and drawing three consecutive games, against Fiorentina, Cesena and Inter. They returned to winning ways in week seven, Chinaglia scoring the only goal against Cagliari, and after the ninth match Lazio shared first place with Juventus and Napoli. A week later, and two days before Christmas, they won at Verona to take sole leadership of *Serie A*. They would not be caught.

Giuseppe Wilson was captain but Chinaglia was the most dominant figure on the pitch. With just six games to go, and with Juventus three points behind them, Maestrelli's team faced lowly Verona in Rome. It should have been a formality but at the interval Lazio were losing 2–1. As soon as referee Luciano Giunti blew for half-time Chinaglia ran into the players' tunnel and shut the Lazio dressing-room door, turning to tell his colleagues, 'Back onto the pitch!' For 10 minutes the entire team waited in the middle of the Olimpico and the crowd signalled their approval of Chinaglia's dramatic gesture by applauding the entire time. His punitive measure worked, Lazio eventually winning 4–2.

During a game at Inter, and in front of 80,000 people, Chinaglia kicked team-mate Vincenzo D'Amico up the backside because he was not 'pressing' Sandro Mazzola, Inter's captain and playmaker. 'That incident has become a legend,' explains D'Amico. 'I took it not as a kick up the arse but as a gesture of encouragement. I took it in an affection-ate way. He wanted to encourage me. Everything Giorgio did was done exuberantly. If he patted you on the shoulder people would think he was trying to punch you. He kicked me to move me, that's all it was. I was the baby of the team and it was Giorgio who took me by the hand. He was like a big brother. To other people he appeared dominant and arrogant but he was always good to me. When we went *in ritiro* for the summer he would ask me if I wanted to go with him a day early so we could spend time together.' Chinaglia declined to travel to the tiny village of Abetone, Lazio's *ritiro* destination in the Apennines, with the other players on the coach, preferring to drive there himself in his milk-coloured Jaguar 4200. If he travelled on the same day as the squad he would drive in front of the coach, deliberately revving his engine to emphasise the superior nature of his transport.

On the pitch Chinaglia's brusque style was not always appreciated by his colleagues. Recalls Felice Pulici, 'He thought he was the leader. He would shout and scream at players, shouting what he thought they should have done. Players play with their own instinct and it's not a nice thing to scream and shout at one of your team-mates in front of a full stadium. The one who suffered most was D'Amico. He shouted at him and pushed him because he was the youngest player in the team but it was a stimulation for D'Amico. It had a positive effect.'

Luigi Martini did not approve of Chinaglia's approach either. 'I was friendly with Giorgio but we were different men with different ideas. For instance, if one of our players scored an own-goal I would go up to him, console him and encourage him. Giorgio would want to punch him and shout, "What did you do that for?" It's like soldiers in a war. If one of your men is shot you don't go up to him and say, "You should have avoided the bullets." Giorgio's behaviour on the field left a lot to be desired.'

Martini and Chinaglia infamously clashed in the dressing-room following the second leg of their UEFA Cup match with Swiss club Sion. Lazio had comfortably won the first-leg in Rome 3–0 with Chinaglia scoring all three goals, two of them from the penalty spot. But in the return in Switzerland they played poorly and lost 3–1. Afterwards a row broke out between forward and defender which ended in Martini grabbing hold of a mineral-water bottle, breaking it on the bench and pursuing Chinaglia with it. Two players, Franco Nanni and Renzo Garlaschelli, intervened and a fight was averted. 'Things had not been going too well for a few days. There was tension within the team,' recalls Martini. 'After the game Giorgio abused Garlaschelli, he abused him more than usual. He went over the top. He was shouting and screaming. I picked up the bottle because it was

ARRIVEDERCI SWANSEA

there. I would have picked up whatever came to hand. If it was a shoe instead I would have picked up the shoe. He got the message after that. He calmed down a bit.'

The newspapers began to write about Maestrelli's *spogliatoio caldo* – hot dressing-room – and his *figli ribelli* – rebellious sons. Stories began to emerge that the squad was divided into two clans, one led by Chinaglia and Giuseppe Wilson, the other by Martini and Luciano Re Cecconi. Evidence of the clans could be found at Tor di Quinto where the players divided the changing-room in half. 'Chinaglia and Wilson were on the left and we were on the right,' says Martini. 'The clans just happened. Chinaglia and Wilson were together because they were at Lazio before us, while we came later on.'

Felice Pulici denies animosity between players caused the division. 'Logistically the changing-room could almost be seen as two rooms. After the first training session we had together, one group used one side of the room and another group the other, and we stayed there. It just happened that way. It wasn't because we were enemies. It happened in a natural way.' Those in the Chinaglia and Wilson clan were not allowed to enter the section used by the Martini and Re Cecconi clan and vice versa. Entry into a rival area was not taken politely, as Felice Pulici recalls: 'I stayed on to do some goalkeeper training on my own so when I went into the dressing-room everyone had gone. That afternoon I found Martini in our area and using our hairdryer because their one was broken. I said to him, "You can't be here!" Without thinking I pulled the plug out. He was furious, picked up a bottle of mineral water, smashed it and put the jagged end near my throat. It was a moment of high tension. Then he turned around and left the room. On Sundays, this aggression was channelled against our opponents.'

Some of the players believe the role of the clans has been exagg-erated. 'They were a fantasy,' says Franco Nanni, reputedly in the Martini–Re Cecconi gang. 'I was friendly with everyone and enemies with no one. Yes, some players stuck together. Re Cecconi and Martini were both single and had their way of life [both shared parachuting as a hobby]. Wilson and Chinaglia came from Internapoli so they stuck together. When we finished our football we went our different ways. Talk of factions and fights has been blown out of all proportion. The media made more of it. There were a couple of things but we were young and those things happened.'

Giancarlo Oddi adds, 'You find clans in every team. Youngsters get on with some of their team-mates and not others, but there were never clans on a Sunday.'

The training sessions, much to Chinaglia's relief, consisted of 20 per cent physical exercise and 80 per cent *partitelle*. 'The practice matches were taken very seriously. We used to have more injuries in those games than we did in a proper match,' says Martini. The watchful Maestrelli tried to ensure these practice matches ended in a draw.

There were strong personalities inside the dressing-room but the charismatic coach was able to control and weld them into a formidable unit. After a victory, he engendered a curious post-match celebration. Like a religious benediction he would place his hands on the players' heads. They in turn would make a sign with their hands, the index finger of one hand pressed against the palm of the other. 'Once we put on a jersey on a Sunday we were all for one and one for all. There was no way the opposition was going to touch one of our players,' continues Martini.

It was during 1973–74 that Lazio were given another crack at Europe. The third-place finish the previous season had earned them a UEFA Cup place and after beating Sion in the first round they were drawn to face Bobby Robson's Ipswich Town. Once again the Romans would be involved in a violent and controversial tie with English opponents. The first leg, at Portman Road, was a disaster for Lazio as they sunk 4–0. Trevor Whymark, Ipswich's striker, scored all four goals. Robson feared the Romans would try and intimidate his players in the second leg in Rome. 'They should know we are not assassins,' replied Chinaglia at the time. His remark was made to look foolish as Lazio's fans and players disgraced themselves in one of the most frightening matches European football has seen, with riot police needed to protect the Ipswich players and English journalists inside the Olimpico.

The seeds of trouble were sown three days before the second leg, when Ipswich arrived in Rome. 'When I got off the bus to go to our first training session there were these people from a Roma supporters' club who wanted to thank me and they gave me a plaque for scoring those four goals,' explains Trevor Whymark. 'The plaque basically says thank you for scoring four goals against Lazio!' The story appeared in the newspapers and to use the words of Cyril Lea, then Ipswich's assistant manager, 'It was like a red rag to a bull.' Lazio's players and *tifosi* were incensed and the result was a violent and brutal match which ended with players fighting inside the tunnel after the final whistle.

Few, if anyone, gave Lazio a chance of overturning the four-goal deficit but Renzo Garlaschelli gave them the perfect start, scoring inside the first minute. Chinaglia then made it 2–0 after 26 minutes and Ipswich were reeling. The trouble started when referee Leo van der Kroft awarded Ipswich a penalty. Dozens of Lazio fans tried to storm the pitch. 'When Colin Viljoen placed the ball on the spot one of their players came and moved it. Colin put it back and the ball was moved again. This happened four times,' recalls Cyril Lea.

When Viljoen converted the penalty, celebrating English players found themselves being chased by their opponents. 'I remember going up to Colin to congratulate him,' says Whymark. 'Five Lazio players came after us and started kicking us. We ended up running the length of the field until police came on and restored calm. They were spitting and pushing behind the ref's back. Chinaglia in particular was going berserk. He started kicking our players. I'm pretty sure he even kicked the ref. I would say he was the instigator of things. The guy marking me was punching me in the back and kicking me in the shins.'

Alan Hunter, the Ipswich defender who marked Chinaglia that night, remembers him angrily confronting one of the linesmen for not awarding Lazio a penalty. 'Our goalkeeper, David Best, came for a cross but missed it. I was on the goal-line and I ended up pushing away a Lazio effort with my hand. It was a penalty but it wasn't given. Chinaglia ran over to the linesman and practically head-butted him.

The linesman ran to the half-way line because he was shit-scared. Chinaglia didn't try anything with me but he was having a go at players who would step back and take it, going in late when the other player couldn't defend himself. When he was at New York Cosmos a friend of mine, Dave Clements, was also playing there. Dave and I played in the same Northern Ireland team and when we met up for internationals I'd ask him, "How's that dirty bastard Giorgio Chinaglia? If you get a chance kick him in training for me."'

The last seven minutes of the tie were dramatic. Chinaglia scored twice, the first from the penalty spot and the second, with four minutes left, after he charged David Best who then dropped the ball allowing Chinaglia to roll it over the line. 'Our defenders were good players but Chinaglia got across them a couple of times. He was a very talented centre-forward,' adds Lea. In the dying seconds, as Lazio went for a tie-winning fifth, Ipswich broke clear and substitute David Johnson made it 4-2.

'At the final whistle the police had to fire tear gas into the crowd as we went off. It was every man for himself,' continues Whymark. 'The tunnel had this Perspex roof and people were jumping on top of it.' Police cordoned off the press-box to protect the English journalists while the *tifosi* burned Union Jacks. In the tunnel, Lazio players attacked Best, kicking him to the floor. 'The Italian police were just watching this so three of us waded in to get David out,' says Hunter. 'Bobby Robson was shouting, "Don't retaliate! Don't retaliate!" because if we did the police might also have a go at us.' Chinaglia was praised by the Ipswich players for trying to break up the fighting.

UEFA came down hard on Lazio, fining them £1,400 and banning them from international competition for one season, a decision that would prevent the team competing in the European Cup. 'We were naïve,' says Lea. 'Our players came off in dribs and drabs and that allowed their players to gang up on them in threes and fours. It was a hostile atmosphere and a very, very physical game. The crowd was up for it and the referee wasn't strong.'

The Ipswich party were locked in the dressing-room for an hour and required a police escort from the stadium. 'When we went back to our hotel there were all these Lazio fans there,' says Whymark. 'We decided not to go in and went to a restaurant for a meal. By the time we got back, at about 3 a.m., the crowd had dispersed.'

The Ipswich fiasco was the only blot on what proved to be a glorious season. Lazio were top of *Serie A* at the Christmas break, two points ahead of Juventus and Napoli, and they carried their fine form into the New Year. In February they played Juventus in Rome and won 3–1, Chinaglia scoring one of the best goals of his career, a half-volley which Dino Zoff, Juventus's international goalkeeper, had no chance of stopping. The following month he scored the winner in the Rome derby, a penalty five minutes into the second-half. Chinaglia relished the derby and always seemed to score against Lazio's most fierce rivals, never afraid to provoke the Roma *tifosi* by celebrating in front of their Curva Sud, the Olimpico's southern terrace which was the home of Roma's hard-core supporters. Not surprisingly, Chinaglia became a hate figure for the *Romanisti* and they played their part in convincing him to leave Rome in 1976. 'What I remember most about Giorgio in 1973–74,' says Vincenzo D'Amico, 'was his strength of character and his will to win.'

Italo Cucci, editor of *Corriere dello Sport*, vividly described Chinaglia during that unforgettable season. 'He was a great. He was also a great bringer of havoc. When this instinctive man walked onto the field he transformed himself. His slight hunch disappeared. Those long legs – like pins – would make him fly. Those eyes, light and almost dead, would brighten with wickedness. Above all they would cover the entire pitch. They would send the ball to the right position.' Cucci saw Lazio's 2–0 win over Cesena in Rome (predictably Chinaglia scored) and was overwhelmed by the striker's display. 'He touched the ball in front of his own defence,' Cucci later wrote, 'and sent it over to the midfield. He followed the ball, picked it up at the edge of the opposition's penalty area and shot at goal. I had never seen anything like it. Only one other player could do that, Luigi Riva.'

Lazio constantly kept a three-point cushion between themselves and

Juventus. They could have been crowned champions three weeks before the season ended if they won at Torino and Juventus lost at Milan. Juventus did lose but so did Lazio. They made amends seven days later by beating Foggia thanks to Chinaglia's second-half penalty, appropriately winning *Lo Scudetto* on home soil. 'To win in Rome, in front of our own public and after years of the northern clubs winning *Serie A*, was out of this world,' says Luigi Martini. The players celebrated into the night at Jackie O's, not leaving Rome's most fashionable club until gone 5 a.m.

'That team of 1974 was a fantastic team,' says Felice Pulici. 'We played total football, like Holland. We played so harmoniously. It was a perfect machine. Our defence conceded less goals than any other team, we had a fantastic midfield player in Frustalupi and a forward of high power in Chinaglia. Giorgio was positive in his attitude. He had great strength and could shoot with both feet.'

The team from Rome scored 45 goals that season and the man from Carrara was responsible for more than half of them. His tally of 24, one more than Inter's Roberto Boninsegna, also made him *Serie A capocannoniere* – top scorer. He was the first Lazio player to win the award since Silvio Piola in 1943. 'We won the league well and Giorgio was crucial to us winning the championship,' adds Pulici. 'We suffered the previous year and as a result we were more of a team. We knew what we were doing. It was well calculated. It's difficult to repeat a great championship. I had a fear we could not repeat what we did in 1973 the following year but we did. I was more surprised that we won in 1974 than nearly winning in 1973.'

During this heady period, a former Swansea Town colleague visited Chinaglia in Rome. Roy Saunders saw him play and score in the Rome derby. 'Somewhere along the line after he left Swansea he had a shock!' says Saunders. 'He was a different player, running and looking for positions.' Saunders had left a message with Chinaglia at Lazio's training camp. He told him he was in Rome and which hotel he was staying in. 'He took me out in the evening and showed me around Rome. He was like a god. He used to park his car wherever he wanted.

"They won't book me. I'm Giorgio Chinaglia." We went to a restaurant. There was a band playing and when he came in they stopped playing, walked off the stage and came over to talk to him.'

The 1974–75 season was something of an anticlimax. There was no European Cup and the defence of their title was lukewarm, Lazio finishing fourth, six points behind champions Juventus. Chinaglia received a hostile reception at every away match. The public could not forgive his act of petulance during the World Cup in West Germany after he was substituted in the first match against Haiti. 'He was not liked by other fans because of his attitude and exuberant ways, especially after the World Cup,' says Giancarlo Oddi. 'Whichever stadium he went to he was booed, whistled and cat-called. They went for him hard.'

At one stage Lazio were only four points behind Juventus and challenging for a second title but the turning point came after a 2–1 win in Bologna at the end of March. In the dressing-room afterwards Maestrelli, suddenly gripped by a chill, clung to a radiator for warmth. He underwent tests at a private clinic in Rome, Clinica Paideia, where stomach cancer was diagnosed. The players were informed of his condition a few days later, before the home match with Torino. They were shattered by the news and it showed in their performance, Lazio losing 5–1. Their minds were clearly elsewhere. A fortnight later they lost heavily again, 4–0 away to Juventus. The championship was on its way to Turin once again.

The doctors gave Maestrelli just weeks to live but he did not lose his battle against cancer until November 1976. At one point he appeared to make a miraculous recovery and even returned to coach Lazio a few months into the 1975–76 season. The recovery was illusory. An era was about to end.

Above: Chinaglia (back row, second from right) in a Cardiff Schools line-up, c.1962.

Right: Mario Chinaglia in the kitchen of the Bamboo Room.

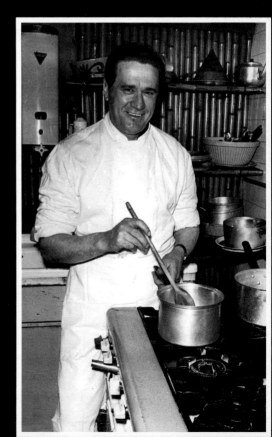

Top: Chinaglia with his friend and Swansea Town team-mate Alan Jones.
bove: Posing for a newspaper during his contract row with Swansea Town, early 196
Chinaglia, whose father wanted him to join an Italian club, packs his suitcase.

In action against Grimsby Tow

Top: Conferring with Juan Carlos Lorenz, his first coach at Lazio, at Roehampton before a Fairs Cup match against Arsenal, 1970.
Above: Two former Swansea Town apprentices clash in the Fairs Cup. Arsenal's John Roberts tackles Chinaglia.

Top: Scoring the penalty against Foggia that won Lazio their first league title, 1974.
Above: Chinaglia (right) embraces Lazio coach Tommaso Maestrelli after the victory over Foggia

Sharing a light moment with Pelé in the New York Cosmos locker-room, 1976.

Above: Celebrating a goal with Cosmos team-mate Franz Beckenbauer.

Left: Commentating for Italian television at the 1998 World Cup finals in France.

CHAPTER NINE

JUNE 16, 1974. The room inside the Nestor Hotel Ludwigsburg, on the outskirts of Stuttgart and the Italians' base during the World Cup, was crammed with Italian journalists. In front of them, and sitting at the head of a long table, was Chinaglia. Over a red T-shirt he was wearing his national team tracksuit, blue with a red, white and green trim along the sleeves. The player, his face unshaven and his hair slightly dishevelled, looked as though he had just got out of bed.

Chinaglia was the subject of a press conference hastily organised by the *Federcalcio* following his behaviour during Italy's opening World Cup match against Haiti the previous evening. Courtesy of the Lazio striker, the tournament had been provided with its first piece of controversy. When, almost 20 minutes from the end and with Italy holding a slender 2–1 lead, Ferruccio Valcareggi decided to replace him with Pietro Anastasi, his rival from Juventus, Chinaglia vented his fury by delivering a *vafanculo*, (the Italian equivalent of 'fuck off') to his coach. Feeling he did not deserve to be substituted he stormed off the field, waving away the Italian bench as he ran straight down the players' tunnel. He broke the door of the dressing-room and then threw eight empty mineral water bottles, which were lined up on a table inside, against the wall.

There was talk Chinaglia would never again play for his country. His

Lazio team-mate and friend, Giuseppe Wilson, who was also in the Italian World Cup squad, had overheard *Federcalcio* officials talk about sending Chinaglia home before the second match against Argentina. All would be forgiven, Chinaglia was told, if he publicly apologised to Valcareggi. Following the advice of Tommaso Maestrelli, who had flown to West Germany to visit the Lazio players in the squad, he reluctantly agreed. Valcareggi was unmoved. 'Chinaglia may blow hot and cold. I am merely cool,' he said. 'It's my job to make team decisions, to remain outside personality clashes. I cannot help what a player feels.' For the second game against the Argentinians, Anastasi would play from the start. Chinaglia was not even named as one of the five substitutes. He would watch from the stands.

That Sunday morning in Ludwigsburg was a far cry from his triumphant debut for the *Azzurri* two years earlier, against Bulgaria. Chinaglia had just helped Lazio win promotion from *Serie B* when Valcareggi named him in the Italian squad for the friendly in Sofia's Stadion Levski. It was the first time a player from the second division had made *la nazionale*. Italy, runners-up in the previous World Cup in Mexico, had just been eliminated from the European Championships, losing to Belgium in the quarter-finals. Valcareggi, who took control of the *Azzurri* after their disastrous showing in the 1966 World Cup, looked for new blood and could not ignore the Lazio striker's 21 goals in 1971–72. 'He had his merits,' says Valcareggi. 'I picked him from *Serie B* because he deserved it. I went to watch him. He was very enthusiastic. I liked what I saw and called him up.'

For the Bulgaria match Chinaglia started on the bench, with Valcareggi fielding Milan's Pierino Prati and Pietro Anastasi in attack. For two years the latter would be his *bête noire* in the national team. Faster and technically superior to Chinaglia, Anastasi was also physically weaker and had an inferior goalscoring record at club level. At half-time, and with Italy a goal down, Chinaglia came on for the ineffective Anastasi and just five minutes into his début he rewarded Valcareggi's faith with an equaliser. 'The first ball I touched I scored,' he remembers. He raced onto a Fabio Capello pass and fired a shot to the left of Rumiancho Goranov's goal. The goalkeeper saved it but Chinaglia managed to tuck the rebound away. Italy drew 1–1. He was picked from the start in the next international, another friendly, this time against Yugoslavia in Turin the following September. He scored Italy's second in the 3–1 win after a pass from Gianni Rivera. Three minutes after his goal there was a sign of things to come, Chinaglia replaced by Anastasi.

The following game, in October, against Luxemburg in their Stade Municipal, was a World Cup qualifier. Most of the 9,500 crowd was Italian, immigrants who had moved to this tiny country to find work. Italy won 4–0 and Chinaglia scored one of his favourite goals in the third minute. There was nothing spectacular about the strike, just the pleasure it gave the Italian 'exiles'. 'As a former immigrant,' said the forward, 'I understood how they felt.' The second qualifying game was against Switzerland in Berne. Valcareggi offered Chinaglia's father, still running the Bamboo Room, an all-expenses-paid trip to Berne to watch his son. Chinaglia senior had to turn him down. 'I told him I couldn't because I have staff problems,' he explained. 'I am looking for a good chef and until I get one I've got to work in the kitchen myself to help out. I'm very disappointed but business has got to come first.' He did not miss much, Italy drawing 0–0 in a boring match.

'Long John' kept his place for the next qualifier, against Turkey in Naples, but 10 minutes into the second half he was replaced yet again by Anastasi. It was a humiliating experience since he had brought Connie to the game, the first time his wife had attended an international. Afterwards he was bitter and understandably so. His attacking partner, the imperious Luigi Riva, had played just as badly, if not worse. He also complained about his team-mates – he had a habit of blaming other players when things were not going well – claiming the midfield restricted his space by pushing up too far. Franco Causio, the Juventus winger, was singled out in particular. 'His crosses were long, high and useless,' said the striker in typically blunt fashion. Despite his height – he stood at six feet two – and his build, Chinaglia was ineffective in the air. This was due to a slight misshape at the back of the neck which restricted its flexibility and meant he struggled to head a ball. In the vital and ill-fated World Cup match against Poland, which Italy needed to win or draw to stay in the competition, he was presented with a fine first-half opportunity to head the ball past Jan Tomaszewski, Poland's extrovert goalkeeper. Instead, he put it high over the bar.

After the Turkey débâcle Chinaglia fell somewhat out of favour. In the next six matches he figured in just one, against World Cup holders Brazil, in Rome, as a second-half substitute for Luigi Riva. He returned to the starting line-up for the friendly against England at Wembley, in November 1973. Chinaglia had not been involved in the last match against England four months earlier in Turin. He had been a dejected spectator among the 50,000 crowd inside the Stadio Comunale and must have had mixed emotions when his rival, Anastasi, scored the first goal in a comfortable 2–0 win.

For the Wembley showdown, Anastasi was injured and that gave Chinaglia the perfect chance to show the English clubs what they had missed seven years earlier when Swansea Town released him on a free transfer. There was concern that his selection would generate an unpleasant atmosphere at Wembley since the forward had played against Ipswich Town in the notorious UEFA Cup clash in Rome seven days earlier. The player himself was unconcerned. 'I know we will get a good reception from the Wembley crowd. They will not try to get their own back for the unfortunate incidents after the Lazio match against Ipswich last week,' he told reporters.

It had been Chinaglia's hat-trick against Ipswich that forced Valcareggi to give him a second chance. 'Now and again,' recalls the former Italy coach, 'Giorgio gave the impression he didn't want to do training. He wasn't very keen on training. He was a happy person and sometimes he gave the impression he didn't take things too seriously.' Italy had never won in England. They had crossed *La Manica* – the English Channel – on three occasions and the best result they achieved was a 2–2 draw at Wembley in 1959. Their first visit was in 1934 when they were world champions and it ended in a 3–2 defeat. It was a physical encounter that became known as 'the Battle of Highbury'. The *Azzurri* returned 15 years later, losing 2–0 at White Hart Lane. 'Although Giorgio was born in Carrara,' continues Valcareggi, 'he saw himself as a former British player. He felt at home when we came to London. He was extremely motivated for this game.'

Chinaglia and the rest of the Italians were looking to make history and they stood a good chance of doing it. England were at a low ebb. Only four weeks earlier they had failed to qualify for the World Cup in West Germany after Poland held them to a 1–1 draw at Wembley. Sir Alf Ramsey, England's long-serving manager, had been heavily criticised for his cautious tactics and for being too loyal to his older players. His departure was imminent. Apart from Bobby Moore, recalled because of an injury to Norman Hunter, and Peter Osgood for Martin Chivers in attack, it was the same English side that had drawn against the Poles – Peter Shilton in goal; Moore, Paul Madeley, Emlyn Hughes and Roy McFarland in defence; Colin Bell, Tony Currie, Martin Peters and Mick Channon in midfield; Osgood and Allan Clarke the two forwards. 'It was a difficult time for the manager,' explains McFarland, playing for Derby County at the time. 'The golden era of 1966 was coming to an end. Alf had been loyal to players like Bobby Moore and Martin Peters. He was stubborn when it came to changing these great players and one can understand that.'

It may have been a cold, damp November night but Wembley was filled to its 100,000 capacity, almost a third of the crowd there to support the *Azzurri*. They witnessed the Lazio forward's finest hour in the national team. 'Giorgio was a powerful and generous player,' says Valcareggi. 'But against England he was even more powerful and generous.' Along with Gianni Rivera and Franco Causio, he was one of Italy's outstanding players that evening. He proved a handful for the English defence, as McFarland recalls: 'His touch was good and so was his movement, especially for a big fellow like him. He stuck out because of his height although he wasn't strong in the air. But his control and movement were very impressive. Italy played well and Giorgio played well.'

Chinaglia created the only goal of the match. With four minutes remaining he received the ball out on the right wing from Fabio Capello. Moore closed him down but he pushed the ball past Moore and then exposed his lack of pace. With his right foot he unleashed a fierce shot-cum-cross, Shilton failed to hold the ball and Capello tapped in the rebound. 'The shot-cross gives you the chance of an own-goal,' recalls Chinaglia. 'I wasn't supposed to play that game. We had just played Ipswich and everyone said a Lazio player shouldn't play. After the goal I had a chance to break away but the referee gave offside. I would have been on my own. That was a good feeling, that win. There were about 30,000 Italians there. It was unbelievable. But for me the nicest moment in the national team was in Luxemburg.'

Before the friendly, one London newspaper drolly advised people not to eat Italian that night 'because all the waiters and cooks would be at Wembley'. The remark had been picked up by goalscorer Capello who, afterwards, took pleasure in telling journalists, 'I dedicate the goal to all the waiters and cooks.' Ramsey would survive one last match, a 0–0 draw in Portugal, while Italy marched on to the World Cup finals, widely tipped to win the tournament for a third time. 'This was the era when Italian teams never gave goals away,' adds McFarland. 'Their structure was based on defence but they had players who could thread the ball through the eye of a needle and forwards who could stick the ball away. It wasn't pressurising football, it was counter-attacking football.'

As for Chinaglia, his outing at Wembley was the first opportunity his old colleagues had had to seeing him play since he left South Wales. Recalls Mal Gilligan, 'There I was watching England–Italy on the telly and thinking, "Is that Giorgio?" It was amazing how he got there. I remember him on the right wing when Bobby Moore went out to him. He knocked the ball past him and left him standing.'

David Summerhayes adds, 'When he left Swansea I thought that was it, he'll be in the Welsh League next. Then a few years later I was watching this game on television and heard his name mentioned and I thought to myself, "What, that big lump? I thought he packed football in!"'

Along with the hosts and Holland, Italy arrived in West Germany favourites to win the competition. They had not lost for two years and one month, they were top of FIFA's world rankings and goalkeeper Dino Zoff had not conceded a goal for 1,097 minutes, a world record. After the win at Wembley Zoff made the front cover of *Newsweek*. The last time he picked the ball out of the net was against the Yugoslavs in September 1972. As an added incentive, the Italian players were on five thousand pounds a man bonus to win the trophy. Drawn in Group Four with Poland, Argentina and Haiti, the *Azzurri* were expected to progress to the second round along with the talented Poles.

News of Chinaglia making Italy's World Cup squad filtered back to Cardiff. Under an article headlined 'BY GIORGIO! IT'S A MIRACLE', the *South Wales Echo* sought the reactions of people who had known him during his younger days. 'He must have come on a ton since he went back to Italy,' said Richie Morgan. 'Really, it's a bit of a miracle,' added Steve Derrett. 'He certainly had flair but he was very temperamental,' explained John Roberts. The man who brought him to Swansea Town, Walter Robbins, was not so surprised. 'He hit the bar once in a Welsh League match at Newport. I thought, "Dear me, he's broken it." I'm not surprised he has got where he has. The potential was always there and he had the physique to go with it.'

With the first match, against Haiti, in Munich and the next two in Stuttgart, the Italians based themselves in Ludwigsburg, a town nine miles north of Stuttgart and an hour from Munich. Their base was the five-star Nestor Hotel Ludwigsburg. 'We were one of the favourites and I was pleased about that,' says Valcareggi. 'A lot of noise was being made about Italy and there were reasons to believe we were favourites because we'd had a good run.'

The backbone of their side were survivors from the last World Cup in Mexico, where the *Azzurri* reached the final, losing 4–1 to a brilliant Brazilian team inspired by Pelé. Four years on and the pillars in defence were Giacinto Facchetti and Tarcisio Burgnich, two Inter stalwarts. In midfield Valcareggi accommodated both Milan's Gianni Rivera and Inter's Sandro Mazzola. It was said these two gifted playmakers could not function in the same team so for the 1970 World Cup the coach devised the *staffetta* – the relay. Mazzola would play one half, Rivera the other. In practice it never worked. Italy played six matches and Rivera's contribution totalled a mere 173 minutes. But now Mazzola would play in an unaccustomed wide position with Rivera in central midfield. Leading the attack was the Cagliari *bomber* Luigi Riva, renowned for his strength, courage and remarkable left foot.

Despite being given the nod over Anastasi against the Haitians, Chinaglia arrived in Ludwigsburg a rather unhappy individual. Two things bothered him. First, he felt Lazio players had been unfairly treated by Valcareggi. Despite winning *Lo Scudetto* there were only three of them in Valcareggi's 22-man squad – Chinaglia, Giuseppe Wilson and Luciano Re Cecconi, and only Chinaglia was a regular choice. 'Our players weren't taken into consideration. I was the only one who was playing and I didn't feel that was right,' says Chinaglia. Until the World Cup the only other *laziale* to have played for Italy was Wilson, in a 0–0 draw with West Germany in Rome the previous February. 'I told Valcareggi he should have picked more Lazio players. If you look at history the team that won the championship had six or seven players in the Italian squad. When we won it was only me, Wilson and Re Cecconi that were called. It's amazing, isn't it? I think Luigi Martini and Mario Frustalupi should have come to Germany. I'm not saying they should have played but they should have been called up.'

The forward was adamant there was a bias toward the northern clubs – Inter, Milan and Juventus – with the northern media, in particular the hugely influential *La Gazzetta dello Sport*, the Milan-based pink daily – pushing relentlessly for their players. 'If we hadn't won the championship we would not have been in the national team,' says Giuseppe Wilson, referring to himself, Chinaglia and Re Cecconi. 'We deserved to be called up before 1974 and some of the Lazio players deserved better attention.'

There were six Lazio players in the 40-strong shortlist but Felice

Pulici, Luigi Martini and Giancarlo Oddi did not make the final 22. 'The blocs dominated the national team and Giorgio had his views about these blocs,' says Martini. 'He resented the fact the northern clubs were dominating the team and he believed the northern players were doing everything not to make him play.'

Valcareggi denies the media had any influence in team affairs. 'I knew the press had a lot to say but I never bought a newspaper and I never read a newspaper. I wasn't interested in what newspapers had to say.'

'Long John' had also been disturbed by Italy's last performance before they flew into Munich, against Austria in Vienna. They had drawn 0–0 but their midfield – containing both Rivera and Mazzola – had been a shambles and the attack non-existent. On the eve of the Haiti game, at 1.30 a.m., Chinaglia paid Valcareggi a visit in his hotel room to discuss the issue of Rivera and Mazzola. 'They shouldn't play together. One or the other should play. They give me the ball and I can score goals,' Chinaglia is reputed to have said. At first Valcareggi thought he was the victim of a practical joke. When he realised the player was serious he lost his temper and ordered him to leave.

Valcareggi claims the encounter never took place. 'It's not true,' he says. 'One day he came in late with a few other players, at midnight, and he said some things he shouldn't have done. That's true. But he never came to my room. I wouldn't allow that and nor would he dare have asked me. That's because I would not have listened to him. He was in no position to tell me anything. He was a player like everyone else and he should have understood how to behave himself.'

Tommaso Maestrelli may have allowed him to sound off at Lazio but the national team was clearly different. 'I don't know what his relationship with Maestrelli was like and I don't know if Maestrelli pampered him or not, but when you come to the national team it's not your club and you can't expect the same treatment you got at your club,' continues Valcareggi. 'At times he said too much. He would speak to journalists who picked his comments up, built on them and things could develop in an unpleasant way. He wasn't a bad character by any means. He just didn't realise that by airing his ideas he wasn't doing himself or the team any good.'

If Chinaglia did confront him about the Mazzola and Rivera situation the coach had not listened. Against Haiti both were picked in the starting eleven. 'They were players with different qualities. Mazzola was more of a forward, Rivera a wing-half. They played together 25 times and did quite well,' says Valcareggi. 'Talk of disagreement within the camp because they were playing was exaggerated.'

In the Olimpiastadion a crowd of 51,000, the vast majority Italians, expected to watch Italy slaughter little Haiti. Mario Chinaglia was not among the crowd. Unable to find cover in the restaurant, he could not afford to close for a week. He was watching Italy's matches on television in Cardiff.

Patronisingly described by one sportswriter as 'calypso men from a Caribbean island', Haiti were supposedly cannon-fodder. Apart from defender and captain Wilner Nazaire, who played for Valenciennes in the French second division, they were a squad made up of amateurs. Their hopes rested on a 26-year-old striker from Port-au-Prince, Emmanuel Sanon, 'the Pelé of Haiti'. A quick, well-built but elegant footballer, he took the islanders to West Germany almost single-handedly, scoring five goals in the qualifying matches. Sanon predicted he would score twice against Italy: 'The Italian defence is too slow for me.' The self-confidence hid nerves. 'Because of the tension we didn't sleep the night before,' he admitted in an interview 26 years later.

Haiti's recent record suggested they could not be taken lightly. To reach the finals they had beaten Mexico. They had also drawn with Chile and Uruguay, both nations that had qualified for the 1974 finals. What they lacked in strength and tactical discipline they made up for in speed and stamina. 'We've been praying for sun,' Haiti coach Antoine Lassy told the Press. And sun they got that Saturday evening in Bavaria. As expected, Italy dominated the first half but Henri Francillon, their impressive goalkeeper, stopped everything Chinaglia and Luigi Riva could throw at him. Chinaglia, in fact, squandered two good chances in the opening 10 minutes.

At half-time the Haitians were holding the World Cup finalists. Then, a minute after the break, the men from Baby Doc's island sensationally struck. With the now-edgy Italians pushing forward for the opening goal, Haiti broke away and scored. Nazaire headed Giacinto Facchetti's cross clear. The ball fell to playmaker Philippe Vorbe, who released Sanon with a brilliantly incisive pass. 'It was a duel of pace and strength between me and Spinosi,' the Haitian later recalled. Sanon sprinted clear of Luciano Spinosi, who unsuccessfully tried to pull him down by tugging his shirt. Sanon then rounded the advancing Dino Zoff and slotted the ball into the empty net. After 1,147 minutes of football the Italian defence had been breached. As for Sanon, the goal changed his life. The next day he turned professional when he signed for Belgian first-division club Beerschot.

Naturally, the startled Italians feared a repeat of their 1966 disaster when they lost to North Korea on an overcast afternoon at Middlesbrough's Ayresome Park. 'We murdered Haiti. I had 30 shots on goal but they scored from a counter-attack,' commented Chinaglia years later. Italy's purgatory lasted six minutes, Gianni Rivera equalising with a shot from the edge of the area. In the 64th minute, Romeo Benetti's deflected shot flew past Francillon.

Five minutes later Chinaglia was given a superb chance to increase the *Azzurri*'s lead. Rivera's pass put him clear of the Haitian defence. He dribbled past Francillon but was forced too far wide for a shot on goal. Expected to square the ball to the unmarked Riva, who had the empty net at his mercy, he selfishly went for glory and missed by some distance, the ball rolling feebly towards the corner flag. Riva, incensed, screamed at him furiously.

Moments later came the substitution and his infamous *vafanculo*. 'At half-time he [Valcareggi] said he was going to take me off after a few minutes. Then we scored two goals and we're winning 2–1 and the son of a bitch took me off,' says Chinaglia. 'If I stayed on I probably would have scored two or three goals. I told Valcareggi to go to hell. *Vafanculo*. That was practically the end of me in the World Cup.' His act of petulance was watched by an estimated television audience of 350 million and to add to his woe Anastasi fired Italy's third in their laboured 3–1 win. Italy's failure to score more goals would prove costly.

After the match the Italians' hotel was besieged by journalists wanting to know the inside-story behind Chinaglia's public gesture at his coach. Andrea Delnero, still in touch with the player at the time, says Chinaglia was angry because Valcareggi had not kept a promise made at half-time. 'It was 0–0 and the coach said, "If we don't score I'll take you out." Giorgio was annoyed because he took him off when they were winning,' says Delnero.

Giuseppe Wilson throws some light on what happened that evening. 'He felt he was substituted at the wrong time, that's why he reacted that way. When he was taken off the team was playing well and he felt he was being cheated, but he should never have done what he did.' (To explain his petulant behaviour, Chinaglia once remarked, 'My problem is I don't know how to be diplomatic. I can't help it. I'm an impulsive person who says what's on his mind and thinks about it afterwards.')

RAI, the national television broadcaster, was anxious the row should not escalate. Its head of sport, Maurizio Barendson, hired a private plane to take Gianni Di Marzio to Germany. 'Baronson knew I had a good relationship with Giorgio and asked me to go over, to see if I could patch things up,' explains Di Marzio.

However unfair the substitution, Chinaglia's behaviour was condemned even by his closest friends. Di Marzio believes the incident in Munich may have started the trend of players publicly undermining the coach. When Napoli striker Andrea Carnevale was substituted during the 1990 World Cup he was caught muttering 'vafanculo' on television replays as he walked off the field and Giuseppe Signori berated Arrigo Sacchi during the 1994 finals when he learned he was not playing in the semi-final against Bulgaria. 'What Giorgio did,' says Di Marzio, 'has certainly not helped to create an exemplary relationship between a coach and his players. No player likes to be substituted, especially in an occasion like the World Cup, but Giorgio should never have done what he did. He was a man of instinct. He scored his goals on instinct and he threw his shirt away on instinct. But it was the wrong thing to do.'

In the hotel after the game the forward found himself ostracised. The only players who talked to him were his Lazio team-mates, Wilson and Re Cecconi. 'What Giorgio did is in the past,' says Valcareggi. 'Everyone knows about it. He did it, the television showed it. It wasn't a nice thing. If he wanted to tell me something he could have told me in the dressing-room. There was no need to gesticulate in that manner. At half-time I told him he might come off. We were going forward and playing well but we needed a player with more speed, who was more lively. Chinaglia was a ram. I needed Anastasi, who was more refined and who gave the team more speed. Chinaglia knew he could be substituted because I told him. If I had made a mistake then he should have accepted my mistake.'

The presence of Maestrelli in Ludwigsburg was taken the wrong way by journalists. The Lazio coach, they wrote, had been flown in by the *Federcalcio* in the early hours of Sunday morning to calm down Chinaglia. Wilson says this was not the case. 'Maestrelli was in Germany but he came by himself, on his own initiative. No one asked him to come over. He came because he wanted to talk to us, his Lazio players. He was our friend and coach.'

By the time of Italy's second match four days later, Chinaglia had made his peace with the Italian management and was not sent home. The English journalist Brian Glanville, covering the tournament for *The Sunday Times*, encountered the forward in Stuttgart before the Argentina match. He asked him about his gesture at Valcareggi. Chinaglia laughed it off. 'Maybe I'm too much like you!' he gruffly replied. (In the early 1970s Glanville was a pariah in Italian football after exposing bribery by Italian clubs in European competition.)

For the match against Argentina, in Stuttgart's Neckarstadion, Chinaglia was not even among the substitutes. Anastasi, who took his goal against Haiti well, partnered with Riva. Valcareggi denies Chinaglia was being punished. 'Without doubt, it was for tactical reasons,' he says. Chinaglia was lucky not to be involved as Italy escaped with a fortunate 1–1 draw. The South Americans dominated the game and went ahead after 20 minutes, Rene Houseman beating

Zoff with a super shot following Carlos Babington's defence-splitting pass.

The *Azzurri's* defects were cruelly highlighted on the night. They were slower, weaker and technically inferior to the Argentinians and Valcareggi's tactic of marking winger Houseman with his attacking midfielder, Fabio Capello, was baffling. After Houseman had scored Valcareggi assigned Romeo Benetti, the Milan hardman known as *l'assassino* – the assassin – to mark him. Using methods not entirely legal, he had more success. It was Benetti who forced the equaliser, pressurising Roberto Perfumo into an own-goal 10 minutes before the break.

Now Italy needed only a draw against Poland to secure a place in the second phase, since the Poles had beaten Argentina in an earlier match. Valcareggi made two significant changes. Chinaglia returned to partner Anastasi, with Riva, disappointing in the previous two games, dropped. Rivera, another huge flop, was also out. Mazzola was moved into the middle with Franco Causio picked on the right wing.

On June 24, on a bright afternoon in Stuttgart, the *Azzurri's* World Cup adventure finally came to an end. They started promisingly, Chinaglia involved in an attack in the opening seconds which nearly ended in an Anastasi goal. But Poland, one of the tournament's most gifted sides, gradually took control and scored twice in a devastating seven-minute spell. Andrzej Szarmach brilliantly headed them in front eight minutes before half-time and then Kazimierz Deyna beat Zoff with an irresistible 25-yard shot. Chinaglia did not come out for the second half, substituted by Roberto Boninsegna. No bad-boy antics this time; he watched the final 45 minutes in the dug-out with Valcareggi.

With four minutes left Fabio Capello pulled one back for the *Azzurri* but it was too late. Argentina had beaten Haiti 4–1, Italy were eliminated on goal difference and Valcareggi's reign came to an end. 'We prepared marvellously well,' he explains. 'Our preparations were magnificent. We had not conceded a goal in 12 consecutive matches. But when we went to the World Cup it did not work for us. Perhaps we should have had the World Cup the year before!'

Controversy accompanied Italy's defeat. A couple of weeks later, in an interview with the Polish newspaper *Zycie Warszawy*, Poland's team manager Kazimier Gorski said 'wealthy supporters of the Italian team' tried to bribe his players at half-time when the Italians were 2–0 down. It did not end with Gorski. In the German tabloid, *Bild*, two Polish players, goalkeeper Jan Tomaszewski and stopper Jerzy Gorgon, claimed they were approached by an Italian as they ran onto the field for the second half. Then in the same newspaper which printed his allegations, Gorski about-turned, saying he had never suggested the Italians had tried to bribe them. And that was the end of the matter.

Chinaglia later revealed he was not surprised by Italy's early exit. He feared the team was not as good as the media made them out to be after that friendly in Vienna. Says Chinaglia, 'During that game I thought, "We're not going anywhere." He [Valcareggi] kept changing and keeping players happy. It became a joke. There was pressure from the clubs as well.' After losing to North Korea in 1966 they were greeted by insults and rotten tomatoes when they arrived at the Christopher Columbus Airport in Genoa. They received the same welcome eight years later, despite secretly switching their landing destination from Milan to Rome.

'The team in 1974 was the strongest Italy had had for 20 years and technically it was the best team in the competition,' says Giuseppe Wilson, who came on as a substitute against Argentina and Poland. 'There weren't any wars between players but there were too many characters who could not blend together on or off the field and it was like a wasting disease, a decay. The problem was that the 22 of us all thought we were stars.' A media inquest opened into Italian football – *catenaccio* was now obsolete, Riva and Rivera had let Valcareggi down, players were out of condition, Valcareggi had been too loyal to certain players. All had an element of truth.

The respected journalist, Giovanni Arpino, neatly summed up Italy's 1974 World Cup: 'For a moment we thought we had got rid of the technical and tactical politics that have weighed down the Italian clan. We made the mistake of dutiful optimism, of believing that at long last certain collective interests would be taken into consideration. The decline was foreseeable and could have been controlled. The old guard of Mexico could not find the strength of years gone by. What has been done to replace them, to build a different national team? Everyone knew this World Cup required speed, concentration, a compact team and athleticism.'

There was talk of disharmony within the Italian camp and that the outspoken Chinaglia was responsible but Wilson defends his former team-mate, saying his behaviour did not affect the team's performance. 'What Giorgio did was one incident. It did not make Italy flop in West Germany. The main factor was the long run without losing beforehand. We went there thinking we were the best but we were totally pumped out. We had beaten England twice, in Turin and London, and we had beaten Brazil in Rome. We got to the World Cup pumped out mentally. It wasn't physical damage, it was psychological.'

Chinaglia, who had made *World Soccer* magazine's Most Disappointing World Cup XI, returned to Italy thinking he would never play for his country again. But he did. Valcareggi's brief replacement, Fulvio Bernadini, picked him on four occasions. Predictably, his first international since the World Cup, a friendly against Norway in Florence, was a difficult experience. The Florentines, renowned for their volatile behaviour, booed him throughout the night. Their jeers relented shortly before the break when Chinaglia scored the second goal in a 4–1 win. That season he was insulted at every match away from home; it seemed the public could not forgive his behaviour in Munich. As Giuseppe Wilson says, 'He paid a high price.'

In a European Championship qualifier against Finland in Helsinki, Chinaglia scored the winner from the penalty spot and his last outing for his country came in Moscow, a 1–0 defeat against the Soviet Union in a friendly in June 1975.

His international career had been short but eventful: a fairytale début; creating the winner at Wembley; and helping his country qualify for a World Cup. But he will always be remembered for those crazy couple of minutes against Haiti. 'That gesture he made to me is something you can't wipe out,' sighs Valcareggi. 'He knows that, I know that. I didn't take him off because I didn't like him. I fielded the players in an equal way. I was allowed to make substitutions and I made substitutions. He didn't like being taken off and he won't forget it. I won't forget it either.'

ARRIVEDERCI SWANSEA

CHAPTER TEN

NOT LONG AFTER Tommaso Maestrelli was diagnosed with terminal cancer, Chinaglia and his wife, Connie, talked about moving to the United States. They first discussed settling permanently in the States in 1973, during Lazio's summer tour of North America. They loved the anonymity, the fact they could walk the streets of American cities without being pestered and taunted. Connie, in particular, was easily upset by the insults from Roma *tifosi* back home.

Leaving Lazio then was inconceivable. Chinaglia was one of Italy's top forwards in 1973 and at £85,000 a year, he was also one of the world's highest-paid footballers. He had just broken into the national team and had a fine chance of playing in the World Cup in West Germany the following year. All that would be thrown away if he emigrated – but two years later circumstances had changed. He had become disenchanted with Rome. Maestrelli was seriously ill, Chinaglia's international career was in tatters following the World Cup fiasco and Lazio's championship team had broken up. Giancarlo Oddi and Mario Frustalupi had both gone to Cesena, and Franco Nanni to Bologna. 'I was 28 and a lot of things happened,' says Chinaglia. 'Things were changing and I didn't like it. I thought I'd try something different and help soccer in the US.'

In April 1975 they finally agreed to buy a property in the States, a

20-room, white stucco mansion in Englewood, New Jersey. One of their neighbours was the actress, Gloria Swanson. That same month Connie and the couple's children, George and Cynthia, waved goodbye to Rome to start a new life on the other side of the Atlantic while Chinaglia stayed in Rome until the end of the season.

While spending the summer at Englewood, Chinaglia was approached by Giuseppe Pinton, a fellow Italian and consultant for a North American Soccer League (NASL) club called Hartford Bicentennials. Pinton, a former Classics teacher from the southern Italian city of Catanzaro, in the Calabria region, wanted the Lazio striker to be a guest player in a friendly against Poland. He agreed, so too did Umberto Lenzini after Hartford agreed to insure Chinaglia for two million dollars. Hartford had expected the game to attract no more than 5,000 people but Chinaglia's presence ensured a crowd of almost 11,000, most of them Italian-Americans.

This was also the year Pelé signed for New York Cosmos and as a result the country went football crazy. Pelé was expected to retire after his final game for his beloved Santos, against Ponte Preta in October 1974, but the Cosmos contract, worth almost five million dollars, would pay off the debts his business ventures in Brazil had accumulated and leave him with plenty besides. Chinaglia now wanted to find a club for himself and put out feelers. Clive Toye, the Cosmos president, soon learned he wanted to join an NASL club. 'You could not be uninterested in someone who scored lots of goals, spoke English and had a home in New Jersey,' recalls Toye, a native of Devon and a former *Daily Express* journalist. 'There was a big Italian population in New York so signing him was a really obvious thing to do.'

Gordon Bradley, the former Sunderland player who was the Cosmos coach in 1975, recalls how the forward arrived at the Yankee Stadium. 'Clive and myself thought that having an Italian soccer player would improve the attendance because there were a lot of Italians living in and around that area. A Yugoslav wouldn't have fitted in, a Pole wouldn't have fitted in, a Frenchman wouldn't have fitted in. But an

Italian would be perfect because of the community. We knew he would bring a big following to the games. We knew Giorgio had an interest in joining us. The word came through. It didn't come through him, it came through friends. You know how these things go.'

When the 1975–76 *Serie A* season began, Bradley flew to Italy to watch Chinaglia play. He went to see Lazio play at Napoli in the San Paolo stadium. 'Lazio won 3–0 and Giorgio scored all three goals,' remembers Bradley. 'I couldn't have seen a better game. I'll never forget the third goal. He broke loose and was going for goal. He was about 35 yards away and this defender, who obviously felt he couldn't catch him, got hold of his shirt. He was holding onto his shirt but Giorgio carried on running and it ended up with his shirt being ripped all the way down the back. Giorgio was still running and you could see his bare back. It was an unusual sight. The goalkeeper came out and he slipped the ball past him. It didn't take me long to realise that this guy could score goals.'

Bradley returned to New York with his glowing report and Steve Ross, the head of Warner Communications, the billion-dollar entertainment company that owned the Cosmos, offered Chinaglia a contract. According to Bradley, the Cosmos' star player, Pelé, had doubts about the Lazio player. Pelé had been an observer at the 1974 World Cup in West Germany and Chinaglia's behaviour against Haiti had not escaped his notice. 'Pelé wasn't over the moon about it. I got the feeling Chinaglia wouldn't have been his first choice,' says Bradley. 'He was a little bit sceptical.'

There was one obstacle to signing Chinaglia – Umberto Lenzini. The striker was under contract at Lazio and the president was reluctant to release a player who still symbolised the club and was the idol of the *Curva Nord* (the north terrace, home of the hardcore Lazio supporters). He refused to sanction the move and, as a sweetener to stay, Chinaglia was allowed to fly to New Jersey every month for four days to visit his family. The transfer to New York Cosmos faded, but only temporarily.

Lenzini had appointed a new coach for the 1975–76 season, little Giulio Corsini. 'Corsini and Giorgio had a bad relationship,' says

Vincenzo D'Amico. Of their many rows the worst occurred a month into the season and a few days before the Rome derby. When Chinaglia told the coach he would be flying to New York the day after the Roma game Corsini replied, 'You are not going to America while I'm coach!' It seemed Lazio had broken their promise and Chinaglia stormed into the dressing-room at Tor di Quinto in tears. When he scored the equaliser in a 1–1 draw Lenzini had no choice but to overrule his coach.

'With his family in America it was obvious he was not the same man,' adds D'Amico. 'His performances were not the same, his play was not the same.'

According to Luigi Martini, 'With Maestrelli gone Giorgio had suddenly lost his guide. Perhaps he did not realise Maestrelli was such an influence until he was not there.'

Lazio started the championship poorly. Two years after winning *Lo Scudetto* they found themselves in a relegation battle and after three months Corsini was fired, replaced by a thinner and frailer Maestrelli who was defying his medical prognosis. 'Corsini and Maestrelli were totally different people,' explains Felice Pulici. 'Maestrelli was a constant referral point for the players. He was a man who had the ability of creating a rapport among all the players. Corsini was a young coach with young ideas. He did not have an ideal rapport with players. Instead he made the players work hard in training.'

Corsini would have little joy elsewhere. In his next job, at Cesena, he lasted only three matches. 'We were very unfair with Corsini,' says Luigi Martini. 'He was a different man with different ideas. But Maestrelli was still alive and we were pining for him. The way we behaved to Corsini was unjust but that was because we loved Maestrelli so much. When he came back he was not the same. The illness had affected him.'

Lazio struggled badly during 1975–76. Maestrelli's return was something of a desperate move by Lenzini since the coach was terminally ill. In March, with Lazio in danger of dropping into *Serie B*, the Cosmos came back looking to sign Chinaglia. By now Gordon

Bradley had been replaced by another Englishman, Ken Furphy. Bradley had paid the price for a mediocre 1975 after the Cosmos failed to make the Soccer Bowl quarter-finals. (The NASL was split into four divisions – Northern, Eastern, Central and Western. Each division had five teams and the top two progressed into the quarter-finals, which were run on a knockout basis. Cosmos played in the Northern division and, despite Pelé's presence, finished third behind Boston Minutemen and Toronto Metro-Croatia.) Born in Stockton-on-Tees, Furphy had been a modest wing-half. Failing to make the grade at Everton he played for Runcorn, Darlington and, as player-manager, Workington Town. One of the first 'tracksuit' managers in English football, he won promotion to the Third Division with Workington in 1964 and, six years later, led second-division club Watford to the semi-finals of the FA Cup. Sacked by Sheffield United in October 1975, Furphy, disenchanted with the English game, had crossed the Atlantic for a new challenge.

'We went on a pre-season tour to San Diego, Dallas, San Antonio, Phoenix and Hawaii,' recalls Furphy. 'We did reasonably well but we obviously needed a striker. Pelé was still a great player but he was 34. I left the matter with Clive Toye and he went out to see who was available. He came back to me and mentioned Chinaglia. To be honest, I'd never heard of him. We didn't get coverage of Italian football in those days. I asked Clive about his record and he said he was an Italian international. He also said he spoke English, which was good, and that he was an Italian. There were millions of Italians in New York. That was a big factor, getting players who were the same nationality as the people living in the area. So I told Clive "Go and get him".'

Chinaglia needed no persuading. His desire to join the Cosmos was as great as it was the previous summer. He issued Lenzini with an ultimatum. This would be his last season at Lazio. Either they sold him to the Cosmos and made some money or, if they refused to do that, he would quit football. 'Giorgio had made it plain to Lenzini that he wanted to go,' recalls Toye. 'If you have a player who wants to go it doesn't put you in a good bargaining position. I didn't know what was happening at Lazio but things were happening at the Cosmos. We were on the move and it was definitely a new challenge for him.' Realising he was going to lose the striker anyway, Lenzini decided to cash in and agreed to the sale. Lazio received $750,000 (just over £300,000) from the Cosmos, meaning Lazio had made a £160,000 profit on Chinaglia. It was good business, since Chinaglia had recently turned 29. Possibly his best days were behind him. 'If Giorgio had not gone in punching and kicking Lenzini would not have let him go. He wasn't eager to release him,' adds Toye, 'because he was still scoring goals. It wasn't a case of, "Take him off my hands" but it wasn't as difficult as signing Pelé. That took us four years.'

Chinaglia played his last-ever *Serie A* match on 25 April. It was in Rome, against the league leaders and champions-elect Torino. It ended 1–1. At the end of the game the huge scoreboard inside the Stadio Olimpico read *Grazie* – Thank you – as Chinaglia waved goodbye to the *tifosi*. But the timing of his adieu was hardly ideal. Lazio were fighting for their *Serie A* lives and there were still three games left.

Chinaglia left Rome for Genoa that night to avoid any possibility of being besieged by supporters at Rome's Leonardo da Vinci airport. From Genoa, he flew to Charles de Gaulle in Paris and then on to New York in a private plane. 'At the start of the season he had already made up his mind that he was going to America,' remembers Felice Pulici. 'At the beginning he didn't want to come back at all. The Roma fans were making life difficult for him, he was having problems with Corsini and Maestrelli was very ill. We were all affected by Maestrelli but Giorgio above all. He was basically Giorgio's father, inside football and out. Although he came back as coach, we all knew he had lost the fight for his life.'

In the end Lazio avoided relegation on the last day and only on goal difference, the 2–2 draw at Como proving just enough, but Chinaglia's desertion at such a critical time was not appreciated by some of his team-mates. 'It wasn't a nice thing to do and it didn't go down well with the fans,' says Luigi Martini. After saving Lazio from relegation, Maestrelli stopped working. He returned to the Paideia Clinic where, from his balcony, he gazed out at Tor di Quinto. He became a reclusive figure and refused to see visitors. The cancer claimed his life in November 1976 and he was buried at Prima Porta cemetery, a distraught Chinaglia one of the pall-bearers.

'His disappearance from life was a tremendous loss not only for us but Italian football. He had great knowledge,' says Felice Pulici.

Chinaglia arrived in New York in time for the Cosmos' sixth game of the season, at home against the Los Angeles Aztecs. 'Chinaglia', said a press release issued by the Boston Minutemen, one of the Cosmos' biggest rivals, 'grew up in Wales, England.'

The ambitious New York club had experienced an indifferent start, losing two of the first five games. They had been missing a target-man. Pelé, by his own admission, was far from being the force he once was. It was hoped the former Lazio forward would score the goals that would crown the Cosmos champions. 'I'll be honest,' says Keith Eddy, one of the club's English players, 'I'd never heard of him, and when we had our first training session with him I wasn't impressed. He arrived in a fanfare. He was this superstar, so maybe I expected too much. But after a while he started knocking in all these goals. He had a huge ego but he was a nice guy. I had this groin injury – it eventually finished my career – and I had to go into hospital. All of a sudden this limousine pulls up outside my house. It was Giorgio coming to take me to the hospital. I lived quite far from his house, around 45 miles away. That's the kind of guy he was.'

The large Italian community in New York now had a hero to cheer at the Yankee Stadium. Charlie Aitken, the former Aston Villa left-back who joined the Cosmos a few months before Chinaglia, recalls, 'The Italians held a Giorgio Chinaglia Night to celebrate him playing for the Cosmos. It was at this hotel on the banks of the River Hudson and it was unbelievable. There must have been more than a thousand people there and they were handing round dustbins – big, black dustbins – to collect money for him. They were stuffing them full of $100 notes and the bins were full to the brim. He didn't bloody need it because he was on much more than myself and the other players! There was masses of food and drink – pasta, salami – all that sort of thing. These Italian men were wearing double-breasted suits with their hair all slicked back. I've never forgotten that night.'

Management gave Furphy the funds to build a side that would dominate the NASL. Not surprisingly, he imported from Britain – midfielder Terry Garbett, winger Tony Field and centre-half Keith Eddy had all played for him at Sheffield United. Charlie Aitken, a Scottish left-back who had clocked up more than 500 games for Aston Villa, was another new arrival, so too was Irish midfielder Dave Clements, who had served Everton well, and the former Wrexham winger Brian Tinnion. There were two interesting South American recruits, the stylish Peruvian midfielder Ramon Mifflin, who had played with distinction for Peru in the 1970 World Cup in Mexico, and Brazilian defender Nelsi Morais. Chinaglia was supposedly the last piece in the jigsaw.

'All goalscorers have an ego,' says Keith Eddy. 'Giorgio didn't brag to his team-mates. It was silly things, like he would talk about himself in the third person – "Chinaglia thinks this, Chinaglia thinks that." I'd say to him, "For Christ's sake, Giorgio, say 'I think!'" I'm sure he didn't realise he was doing it. He had a tremendous amount of adoration in Rome and obviously that's going to have an effect.'

His Cosmos début came on 17 May 1976. More than 24,000 people filled the Yankee Stadium to watch the Cosmos thump the Aztecs, George Best and all, 6–0. Chinaglia scored twice, along with Pelé and Keith Eddy. At the end of the match he and Pelé were given a standing ovation. Chinaglia was proving an inspired buy. In his second game, at Boston, he scored both Cosmos goals in their 2–1 win.

His third game, in Florida against Tampa Bay Rowdies, was a disaster, Chinaglia failing to score in the dismal 5–1 defeat. After just three games he criticised his new employers, claiming they had 'an English third-division mentality'. Ten years after leaving Swansea Town, Chinaglia had clearly still not forgotten his experience of British football. The Cosmos quickly returned to winning ways, beating Minnesota Kicks and Portland Timbers. But it was clear that, despite the enormous sums spent on players, all was not well at the Yankee Stadium. During one Cosmos game, against Toronto Blizzard, a banner fluttered ominously in the breeze sweeping through the upper tier: 'GO HOME KEN FURPHY AND TAKE YOUR BOYS WITH YOU' it read. Furphy's team had a dual identity, the Latin attack – Chinaglia, Pelé, Mifflin – and an English-style back four and midfield – Aitken, Eddy, Garbett, Field and Tinnion. It proved an uncomfortable blend, as the team's erratic results showed.

'The thing I remember most about Giorgio,' continues Furphy, 'was his ability to take shots with his right foot. In training you could rattle balls at him, and I mean repetition shots, and he could take them with his right foot no matter how they came. Pelé couldn't equal him in that. Giorgio could get his instep onto the ball, get it down and then put it into the back of the net. He was so agile on his feet and he could change his body position so well. I was amazed when I saw him doing it.'

Chinaglia went on to become the most prolific NASL marksman of 1976, scoring 19 goals in 19 matches. His finest hour came against Miami Toros in New York when he hit five goals in the Cosmos' 8–2 win. But the Soccer Bowl went to Toronto Metros-Croatia, the Cosmos falling at the quarter-final stage to Tampa Bay Rowdies. 'I'd say Giorgio's heading ability was 60 per cent. It was good enough for that league but I don't know how he would have faired against better centre-halves,' adds Furphy. 'He wasn't overly energetic but he led the line well. His first touch of the ball when he was going in for a shot was brilliant, you cannot argue with that. He was more or less a complete centre-forward. He had an eye for goal and worked hard for the team. I had no problems with him on the field.'

According to Furphy and several of the Cosmos players at the time, behind the mutual respect there was a keen rivalry between Chinaglia and Pelé. 'He wanted the things Pelé was having. He was upset that wherever we went Pelé had a private suite rather than just a bedroom so he wanted a suite,' says Furphy. 'Also Pelé had so many hundreds of shirts with his name on so he could give some away at every game.

When Chinaglia arrived he wanted to do the same. We didn't have any shirts printed for him so we had to get quite a few done. When we faced journalists at press conferences Pelé always attended. On one trip he wasn't there because either his passport or work permit expired, so Chinaglia took his place. I think there was a rivalry, an envy, there.'

Most of Chinaglia's colleagues noticed the competition between the Brazilian and the Italian. Recalls Charlie Aitken, 'I always felt there was a rivalry between them. Everything Pelé wanted, Giorgio wanted. Pelé had the use of the Warner private jet and got millions of dollars from Pepsi Cola to promote their stuff. Giorgio was put out about this.'

Keith Eddy adds, 'Giorgio didn't like the fact he was second fiddle. I said to him, "Giorgio, it's a fact of life. Pelé is the most highly regarded soccer player ever. You're going to have to play number two." I remember his reaction when he found out Franz Beckenbauer was coming to the Cosmos [the former Bayern Munich and West Germany captain signed in 1977, a year after Chinaglia]. He was pissed off. Giorgio said we didn't need him but I guarantee you that going through his mind at the time was, "Here's another one I've got to compete with!" I know when the Beckenbauer story started to break that he didn't like the idea.'

Tony Field sympathised with the former Lazio forward. 'The whole thing was geared up for Pelé, he was the king and I think after a while Giorgio got a little bit sick of it. After all, even though Pelé was the greatest player of all time, when he was playing for the Cosmos he was well past his prime. He didn't have the overall impact on a game that he once did. That's not to say he wasn't a good player, he just wasn't the Pelé we once knew. Giorgio was scoring a lot of goals and he was getting sick of the attention that was given to Pelé. We could tell he didn't like the situation very much and, quite honestly, he couldn't wait for Pelé to retire.' He did not have to wait too long. Pelé waved farewell on 1 October 1977.

Charlie Aitken also recalls tension between Chinaglia and another of the Cosmos' stars, Steve Hunt. Hunt, an English left-winger, was a virtual unknown when he arrived in New York in 1977 but he emerged as one of the best players in the NASL and produced a match-winning performance in the Soccer Bowl final against Seattle Sounders that same year. The blond Hunt made television commercials and had his own fan club.

'Giorgio and Stevie had a bit of a fight one morning. Steve called him something for not giving him the ball and Giorgio shouted something back. It was real argy-bargy,' remembers Aitken. Chinaglia punched Hunt in the jaw. No disciplinary action was taken against Chinaglia even though Eddie Firmani, who had replaced Furphy as coach, witnessed the incident.

'He didn't get on with Steve Hunt,' confirms Firmani, 'and he did hit him in training. That was Giorgio. His Italian temperament got the better of him. Steve was very, very popular but I don't think that had anything to do with it [the fight]. I think it was maybe more about Steve also having a bit of fire in his belly. Maybe Steve didn't pass the ball the way Giorgio would have liked but this happens in training. I don't care what team it is, you'll get two players who will have a go at one another. This happens at every professional club in the world. Two players will clash. They are uptight, they want to play well – there are many reasons. I know Giorgio had bust-ups with one or two players but I sorted all that out.'

'There was a problem between Steve and Giorgio,' adds Aitken. 'Steve was a tremendous player and scored a hell of a lot of goals for us. He was always on the television in New York and was as well-known as Giorgio. I don't think Giorgio liked this. Steve was very popular and they wanted him to stay at the Cosmos. If I remember rightly, they offered him £100,000 a year.' Hunt chose to return to English football, joining Coventry City.

Furphy did not last the 1976 season. In June, little more than half-way through the campaign and after a 3–2 defeat in Washington, he resigned. The results had been inconsistent and some of the players, especially Pelé, were unhappy with Furphy's style of management. Pelé, playing in a midfield role with Chinaglia the lone striker and Mifflin sitting on the bench, accused the manager of being too defensive.

Furphy sensed something was happening behind the scenes when he was summoned to the club' headquarters, the Warner Communications offices in Rockefeller Plaza, after a 5–1 defeat at Tampa Bay. 'I was at home in Long Island when they phoned me. Could I come to the office,' he recalls. 'So I drove into New York and in this meeting with all the Warner people were Pelé and Chinaglia. They had a film of the match and wanted to find out why we lost. I objected to these two players being present but they were there because they were the star players and had an opinion. When they asked Pelé and Chinaglia for their thoughts it was then that I had an indication Chinaglia was behind this meeting. Pelé said "I didn't want to come here." Chinaglia didn't say anything.'

The men discussed the tape until four in the morning. Steve Ross and his vice-presidents thanked Furphy for attending. Furphy, who found the experience distasteful, told them he would not endure another such meeting. 'Then came a game at Washington. It was a dreadful ground, a university field, and you couldn't see from one corner flag to the other because of a mound in the middle of the park,' he adds. 'We had to walk 300 yards to get to the pitch. It was diabolical.'

The Cosmos arrived at the Woodson Stadium on the back of a 4–1 defeat by Chicago Sting. The Washington Diplomats increased the pressure on the man from Stockton. 'The Warner people called another meeting but I refused to go. That was my career over. I said, "Pay me up. I'm off." I couldn't see any future for me there when I was getting all this interference. Afterwards people were telling me that Chinaglia had been stirring things up and that he was involved in getting me to these meetings. I found this so hard to believe. When we beat Minnesota a couple of weeks before the Washington game, Chinaglia scored. He ran 40 yards to come and pick me up off the ground and give me a big hug. So when I heard these little whispers about Chinaglia stirring I didn't believe it. I still don't believe it. I had no complaints about him whatsoever. I was pleased to have him playing for me.'

Clive Toye confirms Chinaglia had been telling tales and remembers one particular day when he told Steve Ross that Furphy did not give team-talks. To the Americans, obsessed with team culture, this was sacrilege. 'Ken didn't give team-talks, he spoke to players person-to-person. Giorgio reported this to Steve who went through the roof. "What do you mean, he doesn't give team-talks?"'

Chinaglia quickly became close friends with the Warner supremo and consequently became the most powerful individual inside the locker-room. Brian Glanville, who visited the Cosmos on several occasions, described him as 'the Grey Eminence' of the New York club. Gordon Bradley, who replaced Furphy, witnessed how close the pair were while discussing team affairs with Ross at the Rockefeller Plaza. 'Steve wanted to see me one time so I went up to his office, I think it was on the 24th floor. We're talking about the future, where we're going, what I thought. Then there was a knock on the door and without anyone saying, "Come in!" Giorgio opens it and walks in. He walked past both of us, went to the bar and poured himself a Chivas Regal. I thought Steve was going to hit the roof but he didn't. I thought, "Wow! How long has this been going on?" because the way it happened led me to believe it was not the first time he'd done this. I didn't like it but there was nothing you could do. You couldn't tell the owner what he should or shouldn't do.'

How this relationship between Ross and Chinaglia grew remains a mystery. 'That was the question everyone was asking. No one knew,' says Toye, who resigned in the middle of the 1977 season because he felt he was no longer running the club. 'When you have one player who is very close to the ultimate boss it's not healthy for the team and the club. I remember Giorgio coming to see me not long after he joined us. He said he wanted $60,000 over the next three years. I told him he couldn't have any more money. He replied, "I'll go and see Steve about it." The next thing he was getting paid more money. He and Steve were extremely close, he had Steve's ear and I don't know how. It was a situation I'd never encountered before or since. We had a joke that Giorgio had his own elevator straight to the executive floor.' (While he was Lazio president in the early 1980s, Chinaglia said of Steve Ross, 'He decided my destiny . . . He became friendly to me and took me under his wing. He was convinced that as a manager I would score as many goals as I did as a player.')

There was another side to the striker, as Furphy discovered before he quit. 'There was a tragic accident in the Italian community when some kids put firecrackers in a hydrant. The glass blew out and killed this little girl,' recalls Furphy. 'Giorgio, who was a hero among the Italians, asked me if we could play a match to raise money for the girl's family. We had a game in two days' time but I agreed. I didn't play the first-choice team but I told Giorgio he and Pelé could play a bit of the game so at least they would be there.'

Despite the newspaper speculation, Chinaglia denied playing a part in Furphy's departure. Keith Eddy, who was one of Chinaglia's close friends at the Cosmos, supports this view: 'I don't think Giorgio had anything to do with it. I think it was more to do with Pelé's situation. Pelé didn't like him. I think the world of Ken but he was very fixed in his ways. When you're coaching players like Pelé you've got to be flexible and I don't think Ken was flexible.'

Whether or not he was involved in applying pressure on Furphy, Chinaglia was glad to see him resign. Chinaglia believed Furphy was one of the reasons for the poor team spirit at the Yankee Stadium. 'Furphy certainly knew his soccer,' said Chinaglia, 'but it didn't make up for what I believed to be his terrible weakness – an inability to get on well with other people.'

Bradley, who had coached the Cosmos the previous year, returned. A competitive midfielder in his playing days and someone who, in 1968, once marked Pelé out of a game between Santos and New York Generals, Bradley was born in Sunderland and began his career with his hometown club before moving to Bradford Park Avenue and then Carlisle United. He moved to the United States in 1968, when the NASL was formed, to play for New York Generals and his association with the Cosmos dated back to 1971, when he was appointed player-coach.

Chinaglia had mixed feelings about Bradley, one of football's 'nice guys'. He found him 'friendly and easy to like' but was not impressed with his knowledge of the game. There, Furphy scored higher. The team immediately responded to Bradley's softer style of management, winning six consecutive matches. This was a good period for the team but a bad one for Chinaglia who had gone seven games without a goal, shades of the 1970–71 season at Lazio. 'We had a chat about why he wasn't scoring,' recalls Keith Eddy. 'We were looking for all sorts of reasons, reasons really that weren't there. All goalscorers have a lean spell. It didn't last long and the goals soon returned.'

It was eighth-time lucky for the striker. He scored twice in the 5–0 win over Washington and then notched up a hat-trick in the 4–0 victory over Dallas Tornado 10 days later. The Cosmos reached the play-offs but lost to Tampa Bay Rowdies. 'I'm convinced the reason he scored all these goals,' adds Eddy, 'was because he virtually didn't have a backlift, so goalkeepers never got the chance to set themselves up for his shots. With a player like me, the whole world knew when I was going to shoot! Giorgio didn't have to wind up and pull his leg into the air. If the ball dropped over his right shoulder – and that was his real strength – he would score. One-on-one with the goalkeeper, he would score. I remember beating Tulsa 9–0 and Giorgio scored six of our goals. You've got to say Pelé was the Cosmos' best buy because of what he did off the field. He gave the American game credibility. But if I had to say who was the best buy when it came to achievements on the pitch, I'd have to say Giorgio Chinaglia. He was the most efficient goalscoring machine I've ever seen.'

If the Cosmos dressing-room in 1976 was football's equivalent of the United Nations, it was a veritable Tower of Babel in 1977. Apart from the German Beckenbauer, the other new arrivals included Brazilian left-back Carlos Alberto, who skippered Brazil's marvellous World Cup-winning side of 1970, the Turkish goalkeeper Erol Yasin and two Yugoslavs, midfielder Vitomir Dimitrijevic and forward Jadranko Topic.

But like Pelé, who was always accompanied by his manager, Professor Julio Mazzei, Chinaglia rarely socialised with his Cosmos team-mates. Whereas most NASL imports were enjoying a well-paid swan-song under the American sun, Chinaglia was a family man with business interests, notably in the construction industry. Keith Eddy remembers once dining with Chinaglia during a trip to Washington. 'We were playing for Team America against Italy [Team America was the NASL's all-star team which played in friendly matches]. We wanted something to eat so we jumped into a cab. Giorgio said to the driver, "Take us to an Italian restaurant." It turned out that the place he took us to was not in the best area of town. When we wanted to leave the restaurant, the doors were locked, which we found a bit strange. When we got outside the streets were deserted. We had no idea where we were. All of a sudden these kids started showing up on street corners. It was very scary. We ended up walking in the middle of the road until finally a cab came along. "Jump in" said the driver. You bet we did!'

In March 1977, a month before the NASL season started, the Cosmos went on a European tour. One of the destinations was Rome, to face Lazio. It was an emotional return for 'Long John', as Eddy recalls. 'We travelled to Rome on the train from Paris because we'd just played Paris St Germain. We were playing cards in one of the carriages and he said to me, "I'm going to get quite a reception at the station." I started taking the piss out of him. "Come off it, Giorgio."' The train arrived at the Stazione Termine in the early hours of the morning, at 5 a.m. 'There must have been around 2,000 people there,' adds Eddy. 'I'm telling you, there were that many. It was like Giorgio was the king of Italy. Women were holding up babies for him to kiss.'

Tony Field also remembers that morning. 'Then I realised he had been a real star at Lazio. I couldn't believe all the people who turned up to see him. I was very impressed.'

The Lazio side of 1977 still contained several players from the *Scudetto*-winning side of three years earlier, but apart from Chinaglia there was another absentee, Luciano Re Cecconi. He had been killed while playing a practical joke in a jewellery shop. Re Cecconi walked in and, with his hand in his pocket, said 'This is a hold up!' The owner pulled out a gun from under the counter and shot him.

Inside the Stadio Olimpico Chinaglia scored the first goal in the Cosmos' 2–1 win, a low, hard drive past Felice Pulici.

Bradley's team started the 1977 NASL season modestly, losing the opening match against Las Vegas Quicksilver. 'We played like a third-division team,' said Chinaglia later. The New York side then beat a poor Team Hawaii and a mediocre Rochester Lancers, but it was clear the Cosmos locker-room was far from happy. Chinaglia and Pelé were at loggerheads, Pelé accusing the Italian of shooting at goal too much.

Chinaglia was having a disappointing time. After his exploits in 1976 he was expected to dominate the goalscorers' chart but half-way through the championship he was well down the list. He was also being booed by a section of the Cosmos support. 'I remember Gordon dropping Giorgio for a match [home to Los Angeles Aztecs]. Steve Ross walked into the dressing-room and he found Giorgio sitting there dressed in normal clothes,' recalls Keith Eddy. 'Steve said, "What's happened?" Giorgio told him he hadn't been picked. "I own the team. Get changed!" said Steve. In fairness to Giorgio he refused, but that was the end of Gordon Bradley. Not long after that he was replaced.'

Bradley lasted another two weeks. Ross ordered him to reinstate Chinaglia and he duly obliged but two defeats followed, 5–3 in Vancouver and 4–1 in Los Angeles. He resigned as coach in the first week of July, after a 3–0 home win over San Jose Earthquake. 'There was a time when Giorgio wasn't doing too well,' remembers Bradley. 'He hadn't scored for something like three games, which was unusual, so I had a one-to-one with him. "I've got a bad back," he said. I told him to have treatment two or three times a day. For one game I gave him the day off. He just wasn't Giorgio. I played Jomo Sono, a South African player we had, instead. We won and Jomo scored. That didn't fit in well with Giorgio and all of a sudden his back was all right. What I did was the right thing but it created a problem between us. There was tension and maybe that led to me going.'

Bradley remained at the club for the rest of the year, as director of player development, before taking over the reins of Washington Diplomats. 'No question, he had a hand in what happened,' adds

Bradley. 'That's why I was bitter towards him and also Steve Ross for allowing it to happen. I thought Steve listened to Giorgio too much and allowed him to do too much. For one match there was this sign inside the ground, 'BRADLEY MUST GO'. I know Giorgio organised that. And we went to this dinner organised for the team by the Italian community. There were a few speeches and I made one thanking everyone for inviting us. When I finished a couple of guys starting booing. I know Giorgio arranged that.'

The Cosmos vacancy was quickly filled by Eddie Firmani, a friend of Chinaglia's, who had recently been coaching Tampa Bay. Chinaglia was seen as the driving force behind the appointment. He denied advising Ross to hire Firmani. His former team-mates, however, are not convinced. 'I'm sure Giorgio had a say in everything,' explains Charlie Aitken. 'He wasn't a player-manager, more of a player-director. No player had more of a say than Giorgio, not even Pelé. I'm sure he had a hand in Firmani arriving. He and Steve Ross always got on and Steve listened to what he said.'

Keith Eddy agrees that Chinaglia was the most influential player at the club. 'To a degree, he was the power behind the throne. He called me at home one night – this is when I was injured – and asked me whether I wanted to be coach. I said, "Giorgio, you're not in a position to ask me if I want to be coach." He said, "Do you want to be coach?" I said I didn't really fancy it. "OK. I'm going to bring in Eddie Firmani." And he did. Giorgio had that power. He had a very big say in the running of the club and we all knew about it. He did have this amazing relationship with Steve Ross and no one ever figured out how it came about. It was like he was Steve's adopted son. I'd come up with all these different versions about why he and Steve were so close but he never told me the reason.'

It was rumoured that Chinaglia had met Firmani in Tampa, at the end of May, while the Cosmos were in Florida for the match against the Rowdies. Five days after that game, which Firmani's side won 4–2, Firmani abruptly and mysteriously resigned with more than half of his two-year contract remaining. Earlier in the season, inside the Cosmos' dressing-room, Chinaglia made an interesting remark to American football writer Paul Gardner, talking of 'a big shake-up, affecting everyone, including maybe me, new people in the front office, you may not like them but something has to be done'. He was also telling his team-mates that Firmani was the new coach well before the official announcement was made on 7 July. He laughed when journalists asked him if Firmani's appointment was down to him. 'No, not really,' said Chinaglia. 'Listen, Eddie was voted the best coach in the NASL last year and the people of Warner's feel they want the best. Of course, if they asked me about Firmani I could only say good things about him.' But Gordon Bradley is convinced it was Chinaglia who brought Firmani to the Meadowlands. 'When Steve told me they were changing coaches, Chinaglia had already spoken to Firmani.'

Firmani himself admits Chinaglia's influence was the 'decisive factor' in him joining the Cosmos. Chinaglia trained with Firmani's Tampa side, in Florida, in the summer of 1976. It was then he first approached Firmani about the Cosmos job. 'He said he would like to come down and train with us so I said that would be fine,' recalls Firmani. 'It's nice and sunny in Florida but I also think he came down to Tampa to get a feel of me. When we were training he asked me if I ever thought of going to New York. I said I'd love to come to New York if the opportunity ever arose. In 1977 the opportunity arose. Giorgio recommended me to Steve Ross. Giorgio probably thought I was the best coach in the NASL [he did] because I put together a team full of young players and we beat the Cosmos every time. They never beat us. No question about it, he played a big part in me going to the Cosmos.'

Known as 'the Golden Turkey' because of his facial jowls, Firmani had won the Soccer Bowl in 1975 in his first year as Tampa Bay coach. When he shook hands with Steve Ross after agreeing to replace Gordon Bradley, he was well aware of Chinaglia's relationship with the owner. 'When he trained with us in Tampa he told me everything that was going on at the club. It's unusual for a player to be close to the owner but the guy just loved Giorgio, I don't know why. They were like father and son. Giorgio had corporate cards, a manager, use of the company's jet – no other player had those privileges. Maybe they would have let Beckenbauer have them if he wanted. I wasn't concerned by Giorgio's relationship with Ross. If he had a good relationship with him then that meant I would be OK. But in the long run it worked to my detriment.'

Born in Cape Town, Firmani made his name as a forward with Charlton Athletic before joining the exodus to Italy in 1955, playing for Sampdoria, Inter and Genoa. While playing in *Serie A* he was picked three times for Italy, qualifying thanks to his Italian grandfather. He returned to Charlton in 1963 and was made player-manager of the Second Division club four years later. He had a mixed time in charge at The Valley. A model professional himself, he insisted his players did not swear or retaliate and threatened them with punishment if they did. Firmani came close to taking the club to the First Division in 1969 when they finished third, but the following year it was a different story – Charlton finished third from bottom and a disillusioned Firmani quit.

He resurrected his career in North America, making Tampa Bay Rowdies one of the strongest teams in the NASL. Chinaglia was one of his admirers. Says Charlie Aitken, 'Giorgio had a lot of respect for Eddie after Tampa Bay beat us in the semi-finals in 1976.' Despite losing his first games, against Seattle Sounders and Rochester Lancers, Firmani brought the Soccer Bowl to New York for the first time since 1972, the Cosmos beating Seattle 2–1 in the final. Chinaglia scored the winner, heading home Steve Hunt's cross 14 minutes from the end.

'At the beginning,' says Firmani, 'Giorgio and I had a good rapport. Everything went so well. The Cosmos were a good side. It was a matter of pulling them together. I made one or two changes and brought a couple of players who didn't see eye-to-eye with Gordon back into the fold. When I was coach Giorgio was scoring three or four goals a game. I knew the way we should play to him. If he got half a chance he would put the ball in the net. No two ways about it, he was one of the best finishers.'

It had been a tortuous year – a lack of goals, jeered by the crowd, the row with Pelé, the Firmani affair and then well beaten in the goalscoring stakes. Chinaglia had scored 15 whereas Los Angeles's Steve David, who finished top scorer, bagged 26. Yet he had won silverware, his first trophy since that magical afternoon with Lazio three years earlier.

CHAPTER ELEVEN

AFTER TWO YEARS in the States, Chinaglia had much to occupy him. He had become involved in the construction industry developing property, owned ten apartments in Manhattan, opened his own soccer camp for aspiring young footballers and would soon buy his own helicopter company. He did promotional work for several companies – Chevrolet, Progresso Foods, Fidelity Union Trust, Pony and Spalding. 'America is the land of opportunity,' he remarked. 'You make money at something for a couple of years then you have to go into something new.'

Influenced by what he had seen at Warner Communications, he was playing the American businessman, the tycoon. He employed a manager and an attorney. He had his own office, above the Cosmos' office, in Rockefeller Plaza. He drank Chivas Regal and drove a '69 Corvette. He lived in a Mediterranean-style mansion, worth a reputed $300,000, which had three acres of gardens, a tennis court and a swimming pool.

On top of all that he was playing for the Cosmos. But his hectic, capitalist lifestyle did not affect his game, as he proved in the 1978 season. Chinaglia spent eight years in the NASL and this was his most successful year, the year he smashed the league's goalscoring record and played a huge part in the New York club retaining the Soccer Bowl.

Chinaglia hit 34 goals in 30 games in the regular season and five in the play-offs, comfortably eclipsing the record of 30 scored by Chicago's John Kowalik and San Diego's Cirilo Fernandez in 1968. Much to his consternation, he failed to win the Most Valuable Player award. That went to Mike Flanagan, New England Teamen's English striker, who scored four fewer goals than Chinaglia.

On the first day of the season, in the 7–0 mauling of Fort Lauderdale, Chinaglia bagged a hat-trick, the first of three that year. In the 30 matches the Cosmos played, the one-time Swansea cast-off failed to score in only eight. He appeared to be relishing life without Pelé, who had retired the previous year. Chinaglia said Pelé's departure would make no difference to the club's success. Who could argue after the Cosmos had won the first seven games, scoring 24 goals?

The club had made new signings, most notably Dennis Tueart, the English winger, from Manchester City; Chinaglia's old friend and team-mate, Giuseppe Wilson from Lazio, and the gifted Yugoslav midfielder, Vladislav Bogicevic, who would create so many of Chinaglia's goals over the next six years. The striker was in no doubt that the Cosmos of 1978 was vastly superior to the 1977 version.

But early in the season, in the tenth game against Memphis Rogues in Memphis's Liberty Bowl, Chinaglia was involved in a bust-up with Firmani. Tony Field, who by then had left the Cosmos to play for Memphis, recalls, 'Cosmos came to town and we beat them 1–0. I scored the winner. About twenty minutes from the end Firmani took off Chinaglia. Chinaglia was as mad as hell. He went straight down the tunnel, kicked the door and was throwing stuff around [shades of Munich 1974]. The people who were looking after the dressing-rooms told me he was going crazy. "That's the last time he's going to take me off!"'

Firmani remembers the incident well. He believes his decision to replace Chinaglia with Fred Grgurev in the second half cost him his friendship with Chinaglia and made him a vulnerable target at the Meadowlands. 'After that,' says Firmani, 'my relationship with him was absolutely zero. That was the beginning of the end.'

Cosmos were a goal down with quarter of an hour left when Firmani made that substitution. 'We started pumping balls into the box and Giorgio was not the best in the air,' explains the former coach. 'Their defenders were just knocking the balls out, so I decided to put on Grgurev, who was very good in the air. As Giorgio came off the field he pointed at me and said, "You've had it." He immediately went to the phone in the dressing-room and called Steve Ross. "Eddie Firmani pulled me off the field."'

Before he made the switch Firmani intended to castigate his players in the dressing-room after the game for not playing to Chinaglia's strengths, but after Chinaglia made that remark he changed his mind. 'I wanted to save Giorgio's face. Because he had something to do with bringing me to New York I felt I owed him something. I was going to hammer the team for playing the way they did. I taught them how to play to Giorgio. I was going to say, "If you don't play with him, I'm not going to put him in the bloody team!" But after Giorgio behaved like he did, I said nothing. He didn't like being substituted. He thought it was a slight on him but that time it wasn't. It was a slight on the other players and I really wanted to have a go at them. What Giorgio did surprised me. It put a strain between both of us and I didn't bother with him after that. I didn't have much feeling for him anymore. I just told him what to do and what not to do. I didn't have a problem because his ego was so big that if you told him something and he thought it would make him a hero he would do it.'

The match in the Liberty Bowl was the first and last time Firmani substituted Chinaglia. 'He should have asked me why I made the change. I would have talked with him and told him the reasons why. But that's not the way he worked,' adds Firmani. 'Instead of being a man and coming to talk it over with me he behaved like a kid. Maybe I should have sat down with him and ironed it out but he wasn't that type. He was hard-headed.'

In the Soccer Bowl final, against Tampa Bay and in front of more than 74,000 people in the Giants Stadium, Chinaglia scored the second goal in his side's 3–1 win, diving at full stretch to head home the rebound from a Steve Hunt shot seconds before half-time. 'He was incredible at finishing,' recalls Phil Woosnam, commissioner of the NASL from 1969–83. 'Goalkeepers weren't safe if he was within 25 yards of their goal. He wasn't a good player in midfield or with his back to goal but I've never seen a better finisher. Not even Pelé was as good.'

Woosnam, an articulate inside-forward for Leyton Orient, West Ham, Aston Villa and Wales, was the driving force of the NASL during the 1970s, watching it grow from five teams in 1969 to 24 in 1979. He arrived in the States in 1967, quitting struggling Villa to take the coaching job at Atlanta Chiefs. The farmer's son from the mid Wales village of Caersws was appointed commissioner after he helped save the NASL from extinction. When twelve of the clubs who began the 1967 season folded due to financial trouble, Woosnam, along with Lamar Hunt, the owner of Dallas Tornado, organised a low-budget, abbreviated season so the five remaining clubs could play in 1969.

'Giorgio was the best finisher of the lot, no question,' adds Woosnam. 'He couldn't do the things Pelé could do. If Pelé had his back to goal the opposition knew they still weren't safe. But there was no one better than Giorgio for hitting at goal. The ball would come to him at all angles and he would hit them on the volley. He would hit them so hard and true you wouldn't believe it. They would go straight into the corner. He was the best finisher the NASL ever had. No one can touch him.

'Giorgio ran with his feet pointing out. When the ball came to him it would automatically hit the side of his foot. That stopped the ball rising, and if it was coming to him at speed – and don't forget they were playing on Astroturf – all he had to do was direct the ball. He automatically got a good contact with it.'

Charlie Aitken has another theory for his incredible strike-rate. 'He had one of the lowest pulse rates ever recorded. His pulse rate was incredibly low. The average is 70–90 and a lot of professional athletes get their pulse down into the 40s but Giorgio's was 32 or 34. It was phenomenal. This meant his heart was doing next to nothing even though he was running about. It meant he had great stamina although I have to say Giorgio wasn't one for running about.'

The commissioner had his run-ins with Chinaglia. He demanded a written apology from the player following an outspoken interview in the magazine *Sports Illustrated*, where he called the Cosmos fans who booed him a 'bunch of idiots'. For good measure, Chinaglia also said he was unhappy with the way NASL was being run. The latter statement angered Woosnam. The written apology never arrived – Chinaglia was never one for backing down – and Woosnam hit him with a $100 fine, a derisory figure.

Woosnam believes his strong personality was the reason why Chinaglia's name was absent for so long from American soccer's Hall of Fame. (The Hall of Fame was launched in 1979 but Chinaglia, the NASL's all-time record goalscorer, was not inducted until 2000.) 'I think some of the Cosmos players resented the fact he went over management to the ownership. Players don't believe in that. Giorgio went one level higher. His friendship with Steve [Ross] grew over time. When he first came over they didn't know each other and the later relationship was tough for everyone else at the club. Steve didn't say, "No, you can't do that" when he should have said it. You can't have a preferential position with players. But Giorgio should be in the Hall of Fame. I don't care what anyone says, he was the best finisher we ever had. This is about statistics, not stories. Forget the personality problems.'

Despite their domestic domination, the Cosmos had still to gain the respect of the rest of the world. As Chinaglia said after the Soccer Bowl triumph, 'In the United States we have nothing left to prove. But around the rest of the world we have a lot to prove. We have to show that we can play with the best teams in the world.' And so Warner, to the fury of Eddie Firmani but with their eye on recouping their investment, came up with a European tour, possibly the most punishing tour ever devised for a football team.

After the NASL season ended the Cosmos spent a month in Europe, playing in West Germany (Bayern Munich, Stuttgart and Freiburg), in England (Chelsea), in Italy (Brescia), in Spain (Atletico Madrid), in Greece (AEK Athens), in Yugoslavia (Red Star Belgrade) and Turkey

(Galatasaray) – nine games in 28 days. Although they beat Atletico and Brescia, and drew with Chelsea, the results on the whole were poor, especially against the German clubs. The Cosmos humiliatingly lost 7–1 to Bayern – 79,000 witnessed Beckenbauer's return – and 6–1 to Stuttgart. Even Freiburg beat them 2–0. Both Firmani and Chinaglia blamed end-of-season fatigue. The Cosmos' quest for global respect suffered a massive knock-back.

By the club's standards, the 1978 season had been quiet and stable but that would soon change. After twelve matches the following season, and despite a fine record of ten wins and two defeats, Firmani was fired and replaced by his assistant Ray Klivecka, a Lithuanian who had become an American citizen. 'There was no reason because they had no reason,' says Firmani. 'When I joined the Cosmos they were averaging crowds of 21,000. When I left it was 42,000. I won two championships and we hardly lost a game. We were winning games by three or four goals.' His demise stemmed from his not playing Francisco Marinho, the newly acquired Brazilian left-back (he dropped Marinho after he broke a curfew the night before a game), and preferring Canadian goalkeeper Jack Brand to Turkey's Erol Yasin. Both decisions displeased the club's Turkish management (Ahmet Ertegun had replaced Clive Toye as president while brother Nesuhi was chairman).

Firmani had, since that afternoon in Memphis, lost an invaluable ally in Chinaglia, someone who could have protected him from the Cosmos 'front office'. Says Firmani, 'Immediately after substituting him I didn't feel my days were numbered because we won the championship. The next year I had a good relationship with all the players – all except Giorgio and he had such a pull with Steve Ross and the board. Have I forgiven Giorgio? Not really. If I see him again I'll say hello but that's it. I'm like an elephant. I never forget.'

Earlier in the 1979 season, on 20 May, the date of a home match against Tulsa Roughnecks, the club rewarded Chinaglia for his extraordinary goalscoring exploits, especially during the previous year, with a day entirely dedicated to its Italian forward, a big American-style thank you for all the goals he had scored. It was known as Giorgio's Day and involved flattering speeches made by the Cosmos management and the unveiling of some special guests, notably the family of Tomasso Maestrelli, bizarrely introduced to Chinaglia on an electric-powered buggy. The match, watched by more than 46,000, ended in a 3–1 win for the home side, with Chinaglia scoring twice.

Yet what should have been a memorable occasion for Chinaglia was spoilt by booing from a large section of the Cosmos support. 'A lot of fans liked Giorgio,' says Tony Field, 'but there were an awful lot who didn't. He was a bit of an enigma. He scored great goals but he missed so many as well. You know, we'd make an attacking move down the field, the ball would come to Giorgio and he'd shoot over the bar or something, and the people in the crowd would be thinking, "What the hell is this?" I saw him miss the simplest goals. Sometimes I couldn't believe he missed. He'd score a good goal on his own, then someone would set him up, all he had to do was knock it in but he'd miss.'

There is also a suggestion that the American public did not appreciate his outspokenness, such as publicly stating that Pelé, in 1977, was not the force he was when he first came to the Cosmos. But Phil Woosnam agrees with Field. 'They would boo at him because if Giorgio needed to do a simple thing in midfield, he didn't do it. He didn't look a good player in midfield and they thought he couldn't play, not realising his job was to just score goals. He couldn't hold the ball up. There was no way Giorgio was going to have two touches.'

Chinaglia had always been booed playing for Lazio at away matches, but the abuse never affected him. He seemed to thrive on the antagonism. The more he was booed, the harder he played. But the jeering inside the Giants Stadium that May afternoon noticeably upset him because home supporters were booing one of their players, a striker who had scored 91 goals since he joined three years ago. During the difficult 1974–75 season, when anti-Chinaglia feeling was at its height in Italy, the only respite came when he played in front of his own, adoring Lazio *tifosi* in the Olimpico. The New Yorkers were a different breed. When he finally received the Most Valuable Player award in 1981, he was asked about the fans who booed him. 'Probably they feel, "How come this Chinaglia has become of such importance to the club? How come he always gets the limelight?"' he replied. 'Some Italians probably resent the fact that I came to the United States. Most of the people won't even know themselves why they boo.'

That season, against Portland Timbers, Chinaglia bagged the six-hundredth goal of his professional career. 'I've scored a lot of goals and people think I'm going to score every game,' he continued. 'But that's not true in soccer. You are going to have some bad times. One of the frustrating parts of soccer in the States is that most people don't understand it. It's difficult for players to accept that, but it's a reality. It's very hard when the fans don't know about things.'

The Cosmos had made further expensive signings. Two Dutchmen arrived at Meadowlands, defender Wim Rijsbergen and midfielder Johan Neeskens, so too had Iranian defender Andranik Eskandarian, the creative Argentinian midfielder Antonio Carbognani and Marinho. But despite these acquisitions the Cosmos failed to retain the Soccer Bowl, losing to Vancouver Whitecaps in the play-offs. That was the end of Ray Klivecka's reign. As for Chinaglia, he failed to make it a hat-trick of goalscoring titles, losing out to Tampa Bay's Argentinian striker, Oscar Fabbiani.

Chinaglia would surely have topped the chart had he not been plagued by a groin injury – the first serious injury of his career – towards the end of the season. He missed three of the last five games including the final at Washington. Going into the last match, Fabbiani needed one more goal to overtake the Cosmos star and his chance of taking the goalscoring title increased drastically when Chinaglia, concerned about his groin, decided not to play against the Diplomats. The Astroturf at the Robert F. Kennedy was blotted with puddles caused by heavy rain. With his eyes on the play-offs, Chinaglia decided it was not worth the risk. But in Detroit, Fabbiani duly took the crown, scoring Tampa Bay's goal in their 2–1 defeat.

Chinaglia and the Cosmos bounced back the following year. Despite yet another change of manager, Hennes Weisweiler replacing Professor

Julio Mazzei, one-time constant companion of Pelé, the club won its fourth Soccer Bowl in five years, easily beating Fort Lauderdale 3–0 in the final. Chinaglia scored twice and established himself as the NASL's leading marksman with 32 goals in 32 games during the regular season.

Luring Weisweiler – known as WW – across the Atlantic was seen as quite a coup. The German, a disciple of the great Sepp Herberger, made a name for himself at Borussia Mönchengladbach, winning the UEFA Cup in 1975 but, more significantly, he turned the Bokelberg into a *fussballschule*, nurturing players such as Gunter Netzer, Jupp Heynckes, Rainer Bonhof and Berti Vogts.

At first Chinaglia was a supporter of Weisweiler. The new coach, an advocate of teamplay, said his Cosmos would be 'a team without stars'. Chinaglia was in agreement. 'No more big fees for name players,' he warned. The Soccer Bowl was won in the German's first season, thanks largely to Chinaglia's prodigious strike-rate. But at the beginning of 1981, in pursuit of his 'no stars' policy, Weisweiler exiled Carlos Alberto and Johan Neeskens. The German was accused of playing a dull brand of football, the crowds at the Giants Stadium fell alarmingly, dropping from 40,000 at the start of the season to 27,000 at the end, and Weisweiler's name was booed at every home match.

The Cosmos reached another Soccer Bowl final but lost to Chicago Sting in a penalty shoot-out. Chinaglia, who scored five of the Cosmos' eight goals in the two semi-final matches against Fort Lauderdale, was marked out of the match by Chicago's Haitian defender Frantz Mathieu. After that defeat Chinaglia, once an ally of WW, turned on the German, publicly vowing never to play for the Cosmos again while Weisweiler was in charge. He also threatened to miss the Cosmos' annual post-season tour if there was no change. The board admonished the striker: 'It was not for a player to decide who was to be the coach of the team.' This forced many a wry smile since it was common knowledge that Chinaglia had been involved in the hiring and firing of Ken Furphy, Gordon Bradley and Eddie Firmani. But it was Chinaglia who won, Weisweiler heading to Switzerland to coach Grasshoppers Zurich.

By now the NASL was in a critical state. The boom following Pelé's arrival had passed. Crowds at every venue were in decline. Five clubs closed in 1981 – Atlanta, Detroit, Houston, Rochester and Memphis. The emergence of one new club, Calgary Bloomers, was a small consolation. For the Soccer Bowl final, the showpiece event, only 36,791 turned up at Toronto's 54,472-capacity Exhibition Stadium to watch Chicago beat the Cosmos. One Toronto newspaper described the game as 'a non event'. Another said it had all the importance of 'a lawn bowling tournament'.

It became worse in 1982. The number of NASL clubs plunged from 21 to 14. One of the clubs to disappear was, ominously, Dallas Tornado, one of the league's founding clubs and backed by oil million-aire Lamar Hunt. The alarming decline of the league overshadowed another fine season for Chinaglia whose goals helped the Cosmos, once more under the guidance of Julio Mazzei, win their fourth Soccer Bowl title in five years. After hitting the Soccer Bowl final winner against Seattle Sounders, the striker turned on his critics. 'This may sound presumptuous of me,' he said, 'but I have a right to say this goal showed up critics who are saying that I am old and slow.' Even at 35 he was still the league's best marksman. His 20 goals and 15 assists won him the top goalscorer's award for the fifth time, pipping Chicago's German striker Karl-Heinz Granitza.

Some clubs, such as Chicago, were reporting a 50 per cent drop in attendances. The crisis spread to the Giants Stadium, despite the club's recent successes and big-name players. In 1978 the average crowd at Meadowlands was almost 48,000. By 1982 that had plummeted to just under 29,000. For the first time since Pelé signed the average had dipped below the 30,000 mark. 'I want soccer to succeed in the States for a personal reason,' remarked Chinaglia in 1981. 'That's because I live here and I want to see soccer when I'm finished.' It appeared the battle had been lost.

Dull football, economic depression and rising ticket prices were blamed for the dire state of the NASL. 'We weren't getting on television,' explains Ken Furphy, who coached Detroit Express and

Washington Diplomats after parting company with the Cosmos. 'We couldn't hit the big one – NBC. The clubs weren't making any money. They were paying big wages to players and had to fly long distances for games. You can imagine how much it cost to fly 24 people 4,000 miles to California and there was the accommodation as well.'

Against this bleak backdrop Chinaglia looked for a new challenge. Almost inevitably his gaze turned to the Eternal City and to his old club, Lazio. In 1980 the club was relegated to *Serie B*, along with Milan, as punishment for its part in a betting and bribes scandal that rocked the Italian game. Some of the Lazio players, including Chinaglia's close friend, Giuseppe Wilson, had been dabbling in what the Italians call *Totonero*, the black market football pools.

But in 1982–83 the Romans were looking good for a return to *Serie A*. Halfway through the season, in December and while promoting Atari video games in Italy – Atari was a Warner Communications product – Chinaglia spent a day's training with Lazio and 10,000 *tifosi* turned up to provide him with an ecstatic reception. The club president, Gian Casoni, offered him the job of chief executive. The lure was a £200,000-a-year salary and a six-year contract. Chinaglia returned to New Jersey to think about Casoni's offer. There he met with Vittorio Galli, Lazio's vice-president, who tried to convince him to take the job. He refused, saying he had one more playing year left in him, much to the relief of those still trying to champion the game in the States. He announced his decision to stay at Meadowlands just before the Cosmos left for Freeport, Bahamas, where the club had their pre-season training camp.

Chinaglia's shot, so hard it once broke a goalpost, was not as potent as it once was. He had also lost a yard in pace, but he was still the league's top attraction and invaluable to his club. 'He's the first to admit he's not the same player he used to be but he's still a great technician,' said Julio Mazzei. 'He's the kind of guy who stays for 90 minutes in the penalty box, waiting for passes or for rebounds, with someone always kicking at his ankles and someone else breathing down his neck, never giving up, never being afraid of anyone. It's not easy. His kind are disappearing.'

Considering the start he made to the 1983 season, Chinaglia's decision to carry on playing looked like the right one. He scored 10 goals in his first six matches. 'What a great way to start the season,' he said after hitting a hat-trick in the 3–2 win over Tulsa Roughnecks in the Giants Stadium. 'The thought of retirement is the furthest thing from my mind.' Then came the first serious injury of his professional career, a hint that perhaps time was catching up with him. Against Team America at the start of July, he suffered a pulled hamstring which sidelined him for almost two months. His incredible run of 222 straight games came to an end.

He decided to return to his first love. Lazio had been promoted, Casoni wanted to sell and, more significantly, football in the States was dying. The Cosmos, the nation's flagship club, was losing millions of dollars each year. Its owners, Warner Communications, had just lost $285 million thanks to the disastrous performance of Atari, its video game branch. In every corner of the States club owners were pulling the plug. Jacksonville Teamen went, so too did Edmonton Drillers and Portland Timbers. Only twelve clubs contested the 1983 championship and nine the following year, making the NASL's death almost unavoidable.

Chinaglia's final appearance for the Cosmos came on 12 September 1983, in a 1–0 play-off defeat in Montreal's Olympic Stadium. In eight years in the NASL he had scored a record 243 goals in 256 games. Many great players came to North America to see out their careers – Eusebio, Johann Cruyff, Gerd Muller – but none came close to matching his achievements. At the end of 1984, while he was running Lazio, he was also appointed – somewhat inevitably – president of the Cosmos. He had become the president of two worlds. By the time Chinaglia replaced Ahmet Ertegun, the club, losing four to five million dollars a year, had become a poisoned chalice.

Chinaglia ended up administering the last rites. In 1985, the Cosmos failed to pay the $250,000 performance bond, a fee paid to the league for the club to take part in the forthcoming season. Chinaglia was summoned to a hearing at the NASL's headquarters on Broadway.

Clive Toye, who had become the league's president in December 1984, recalls, 'In accordance with the NASL constitution, a hearing was held. Charges were made against the Cosmos and Chinaglia threatened to throw the league's lawyer out of the window. Charming man, as always. A vote was taken and the Cosmos were kicked out of the league.'

The suspension of the Cosmos, says Toye, was the final nail in the NASL coffin. 'When Chinaglia failed to put up his money, that led to others not putting up their money. It affected the league enormously. I was trying to interest some people in staying and some people coming in, and the fact the Cosmos failed to post their bond was very significant. If Manchester United said they were not playing in England that would have an effect on the English league. The Cosmos were the Cosmos.' There would be no 1985 season. The NASL folded, some blamed the rising costs, others blamed FIFA's decision not to award the 1986 World Cup to the United States.

The lure of Lazio – the chance to return as president and bring back the glory days of 1974 – proved impossible to resist. It was certainly a challenge. Lazio had returned its former position as the city's second club. Roma, with a team that included the Brazilian stars Cerezo and Falcao as well as the dynamic Italian international winger Bruno Conti, had just won the *Serie A* Championship for the second time in their history, while the sky-blue half of Rome had been wallowing in the second division for three years. But now Lazio had returned to the top flight, finishing runners-up to Milan. 'He could see Lazio were winning *Serie B* and on their way to *Serie A*,' says Felice Pulici, who Chinaglia appointed vice-president. 'He thought, "They're up, let's go back and make things work again." He wanted to apply the management experience he had acquired at the Cosmos and apply that at Lazio. It showed how much he loved Lazio and that when he left he didn't really want to go. Another factor was that although Giorgio had faith in the NASL he could see there was no future there. It had no roots, it did not mature.'

To own the club he had played for with such distinction, Chinaglia paid almost five million pounds. He would later describe buying Lazio as 'the biggest mistake of my life, because I lost a lot of money'. During his ill-fated presidency the club fell from *Serie A* to the depths of *Serie B*. But the acquisition showed he had never lost affection for Lazio, despite the energy he had devoted to the Cosmos and his efforts to move up the ladder at Warner Communications. 'I bought Lazio,' says Chinaglia, 'because of ego, because of heart. My father said, "Don't buy it! Don't buy it!" He was right.'

When the club's new president surfaced from the arrivals lounge of Leonardo da Vinci airport he was besieged by ecstatic *tifosi*, as he had been at the Termine railway station six years earlier when visiting Rome with the Cosmos. The prodigal son had returned, not for three days as was the case in 1977, but for good. He said he wanted to be the fans' president, 'to give the club back to the fans'. His heart, he added, had never left Lazio. People tried to embrace him and one draped a blue and white scarf around his neck. As one writer commented, he returned to Rome 'as if he was Caesar'. But lifelong Lazio fan Franco Melli, a sportswriter for *Corriere della Sera*, a national daily newspaper, was less impressed. 'His best friends were whisky and Marlboro cigarettes,' he later wrote. 'He had aged. He was just a mask, like a Shakespearean mask in a storm from *The Tempest*.'

As he was driven into the city from the airport Chinaglia noticed graffiti on the walls, written by Roma *tifosi*. '*Sapete perche e gobbo Chinaglia?*' – Do you know why Chinaglia is a hunchback? – said one. '*Perche se fosse stato dritto, non avrebbe preso la Lazio*' – Because if he was upright he would not have bought Lazio. It was a play on words, *dritto* means shrewd as well as upright. Another read '*Chinaglia, undici immobili non dichiariti!*' – Chinaglia has not declared his eleven properties to the taxman. Another play on words, *immobili* can also mean immovables, a derogatory remark aimed at his players.

His home symbolised his position in Roman life. He acquired a residence in the prestigious heart of the historic centre, at the Piazza di Spagna, the Spanish Steps. Referring to his desire for such a property, Chinaglia remarked, 'They said to me, "Impossible! You can't find it!" I said, "Have faith."' From the roof, the grey dome of St Peter's was clearly visible. His wife and children – now they had three – remained in the States. (Towards the end of his Lazio presidency, Chinaglia revealed, 'For many years Connie and I had not been able to go and see the ocean and hug one another. We now spend more hours ringing one another from one continent to the other, than being together. I have made her suffer too much because of Lazio and the Cosmos'.)

Lazio had finished runners-up in *Serie B* to Milan in 1982–83. The coach was Giovanni Morrone, a Lazio player when Chinaglia arrived from Internapoli. Morrone was not Chinaglia's ideal man. The new president wanted Luis Vinicio, the man he learned so much from in Naples but 'the Lion' could not be tempted to return to the turbulent football world alongside the Tiber. Vinicio had coached Lazio before. Hired in 1976, not long after Chinaglia moved to New Jersey, he survived the first season but not the second, one of many fine managers to have been chewed up and spat out of Rome.

So Chinaglia stuck with Morrone. He also surrounded himself with familiar faces: Pulici was his right-hand man and Roberto Lovati, assistant manager during the Maestrelli era, was made a senior official. But he inherited the club in a poor state. The three years in *Serie B* had taken a toll. Lazio had debts of £12 million. 'The football club had no credibility,' said Chinaglia, 'and its reputation with the authorities was zero.'

Lazio had not paid suppliers for ten years. It had amassed debts with restaurants where the players ate. Its takings were gobbled up by the bank as soon as they were deposited. According to Felice Pulici, when he agreed to take over the presidency, Chinaglia was not aware of the critical situation. 'He was enticed into coming back and he wasn't given the real facts by someone who was behind the scenes,' says Pulici. 'He went in blindfolded. Giorgio wanted to recreate the great Lazio but he wasn't given the full picture of what he was going to encounter. People told him one thing when really it was another. There were money problems. When the situation became critical and we needed resources we didn't have any.'

Chinaglia had promised two big signings for the 1983–84 season but was forced to keep faith with the bulk of the promotion-winning side. He did import Brazilian midfielder Batista, famously kicked in the groin by a frustrated Maradona during the 1982 World Cup, and Brian Laudrup, a promising Danish forward, was loaned from Juventus. Then there was another boost when Bruno Giordano, Lazio's star striker who was coveted by bigger clubs such as Milan, Inter and Juventus, decided to remain at the Olimpico following the takeover.

However, the season was a tortuous one as Lazio struggled among the élite. Laudrup found it difficult to adjust. He joked that he learned eight words in Italian – 'the days of the week and how to order a cup of coffee'. Giordano, their international forward whose goals won them promotion from *Serie B*, broke his leg on New Year's Eve in a 2–0 defeat at Ascoli. Chinaglia sacked Morrone after twelve dismal matches. 'Morrone was very knowledgeable,' says Pulici, 'but he was inexperienced when it came to coaching. Results didn't go his way.'

The replacement was Paolo Carosi although Chinaglia had talked of hiring Luigi Radice, the coach who won Torino the league title in 1976. His first match, against Udinese at the Olimpico, ended in violent scenes involving the home supporters. After watching Lazio surrender a 2–0 lead to draw 2–2 their patience snapped. They turned on the players and the journalists in the press-box, pelting them with missiles. One frightened radio commentator told his audience, 'They think it's our fault. I will have to go off the air. It's too dangerous to continue.'

There was talk of Chinaglia making a comeback at centre-forward but the rumour was swiftly quashed. 'Unfortunately I'm 38 and I can't play anymore,' he said. 'I don't want to play anymore. It's a strange thing that I don't miss it at all. Because I'm so much involved with it, I'm playing for 11 guys. When we win or draw it's a great feeling. I thought scoring a goal was the maximum but this surpasses it.'

Carosi kept Lazio in *Serie A*, but only just. On the last day of the season they travelled to fellow strugglers Pisa, needing a point to survive. They drew 2–2. 'Giorgio paid £15,000 from his own pocket to hire coaches so as many Lazio supporters as possible could go to that match,' recalls Alan Wilkins. Years later Chinaglia remembers his largesse with satisfaction: 'Do you know how many people we took up to Pisa? We took 22,000. That's a lot of people.' By staying in *Serie A* Chinaglia could hold on to the club's two most valuable assets, Giordano and the talented defender Lionello Manfredonia, who had both been linked with Juventus.

The following season was disastrous. Chinaglia had tasted relegation with the club as a player and now as its president. Lazio finished last but one, ten points adrift of safety. Carosi was sacked after two league games, the 5–0 defeat against Udinese in Udine the last straw as far as Chinaglia was concerned. Giancarlo Oddi, who was Lazio's assistant coach at the time, recalls, 'I thought we put up a good team. I thought we would challenge for a place in the UEFA Cup, but that didn't turn out to be the case. We had a lot of bad luck and halfway through the season we knew we were going down. Carosi was sacked because we didn't qualify for the next round of the Coppa Italia, then we lost at home against Fiorentina and then lost by five goals at Udinese.'

For a replacement Chinaglia called his old mentor, Juan Carlos Lorenzo, who had recently been working in Mexican football. But 'Don Juan' failed to turn the team's fortunes around. If anything, Lazio were worse and with ten matches remaining Lorenzo was fired with Oddi taking over the reins. According to Vincenzo D'Amico, who at the time was in his second spell with Lazio as a player, the appointment of Lorenzo was Chinaglia's biggest mistake as president. 'Lorenzo was a man who had been away from the scene for so many years. Compared to the 1960s when he was previously in charge, Lazio was totally different. It was Lorenzo who took us into *Serie B*. If he stuck with Carosi my belief is that Lazio would not have been relegated.'

Felice Pulici agrees that Lorenzo was the wrong appointment. 'He was a terrible choice. He was a coach of old. He had left Europe a long time ago and gone to South America. As far as *Serie A* was concerned, he was not an up-to-date coach.'

Chinaglia later admitted that hiring Lorenzo was 'the last lifeline to safety'. Oddi, who continued to work under 'Don Juan' after Carosi's dismissal, says, 'Lorenzo was a great manager and personality but for many years he had been outside Italian football. He was not in touch with the players. When he was previously at Lazio he was paid more than them. When he came back they were better paid than him. He never overcame the situation and we went down like a stone.'

The words of 'Bob' Lovati, uttered before the season commenced, were prophetic: 'We are like a man who has a fur coat. But he needs a raincoat, a pair of shoes.' In other words, it was all very well having Giordano, Manfredonia and Laudrup but other players were needed. 'With Carosi as coach,' continues D'Amico, 'we were doing discreet things but Giorgio decided to change and perhaps he should not have changed.'

Felice Pulici adds, 'Giorgio's choice of managers was more bad luck than incompetence.'

Lazio won only two games all season, both in Rome, against Como and Cremonese. It was one of the blackest years in the history of the club and the two big-name foreign players, Laudrup and Batista, were heavily criticised. 'Laudrup was a great player, as he later proved,' explains Giancarlo Oddi, 'but he was only 19 when he was with us. He did reasonably well in his first year, not so well the next because everything went wrong that year. As for Batista, he was a good player but he liked life outside football. He didn't concentrate on his football and he didn't get many goals for us.'

Both Laudrup and Batista departed Rome that depressing summer. Chinaglia also lost his prized assets, Giordano and Manfredonia, who were, at the end of the 1984–85 season, *svincolati* – free agents. 'It's difficult to judge what went wrong,' continues Oddi. 'As I said, I thought we could challenge for a UEFA Cup place. If everyone knew what was going wrong then no one would be relegated. Sometimes you put out a big team and it does very well, other times you put out a big team and nothing happens for you. Giorgio brought great impetus with him and a will to succeed but unfortunately in football that's not enough. We needed more resources, resources that Giorgio never had. Not only did we not have the money but then the crowds started to dwindle. Lazio has never been a wealthy club but we always filled the stadium. We weren't even doing that anymore.'

To haul Lazio out of *Serie B*, Chinaglia engaged the quietly spoken

Luigi Simoni. He saw Simoni, who had just won the *Serie B* championship with Pisa, as the ideal coach. 'Never would I have believed that I would have paid back so badly all the fans who loved me so much,' said Chinaglia, after relegation. In an attempt to be upbeat, he added, 'We are in *Serie B* but we'll resolve things. The sky is the same colour as our shirts. Someone who is falling down the stairs, sooner or later he will reach the landing.' By November the team was in the bottom half of *Serie B*. Relegation to *Serie C* was a real possibility. 'There were rumours that Coca Cola were going to be involved with Lazio but it never happened,' recalls Oddi. 'The team didn't do too well, we dropped into *Serie B* and these people from America disappeared.'

Vincenzo D'Amico believes Chinaglia was let down after he bought Lazio. 'He never received the help a lot of sources had promised him,' he remarks. 'It was a pity because I think he would have made a great president. A lot of promises were made to him. His American friends said they would put money in but he found himself on his own. He was abandoned, he suffered and Lazio went through a bad time.'

On 3 December 1985, at the club's offices in Via Col di Lana, a tearful Chinaglia announced he was selling Lazio. The club, he revealed, was almost £15 million in debt and facing bankruptcy. 'If we had lost another day,' he told journalists, 'we would have to shut up shop. We would never have been able to pay salaries for the month of December. Lazio has debts with everyone.' The buyer, at first anonymous, was Gianmarco Calleri, a 46-year-old businessman and former footballer. 'I'm convinced in three years' time,' continued Chinaglia, crying openly, 'Lazio will find the place it merits in the aristocracy of football.'

Three days later he was on a plane to New York, his reign as president over. When he bought Lazio he said he had studied business management at 'the University of Cosmos'. He had obviously not learned enough. 'At the end there was nothing there,' says Felice Pulici. 'There was no new income. He never wanted to sell the club but it was inevitable. He had no choice.'

Many of his old Lazio colleagues observed his ill-fated presidency with interest. One of them was Luigi Martini, who suggests he was not suited to the role of president. 'Giorgio was a highly charged person. He did things there and then. When you're a president you have to be more pragmatic. To be a player on the field and a president of the club are two different things. The one does not go with the other. He went there as president and wanted to do everything himself, just like when he was a forward. Instead, he needed to consult with fully qualified people. If you consult with someone else you minimise the possibility of making a mistake.'

Giancarlo Oddi believes Chinaglia should have hired an experienced *dirigente* – general manager – who could organise the coaching staff and deal in the transfer market. 'His second-in-command was Felice Pulici but Felice was just as inexperienced as Giorgio. One was as raw as the other.'

Lazio finished the 1984–85 season in twelfth place. They had to wait until 1988 to return to *Serie A* although their place among the aristocracy took much longer than the three years Chinaglia envisaged. Says Giancarlo Oddi, 'The fans remembered him as a player. When he came from America they had big expectations. In Italy if someone emigrates to America and comes back rich, they have kudos.'

For the second time in his life, Giorgio Chinaglia left Italy for New York, only to return to Rome in the 1990s to work as a television analyst for the sport that transformed him from a £20-a-week Swansea Town player into a millionaire who scored goals on every continent.

Oddi says, 'When he sold up and went back to the United States, his image and personality was dented. But he stayed away for a few years, came back and slowly started working on television. He reinvented his image and the Lazio supporters have given him their hearts again.'

EPILOGUE

TODAY, GIORGIO CHINAGLIA lives in Rome with his second wife, Angela Caciotto. They married in 1985 and have two children – Donald, 17, and Anthony, 14. The former striker left New York for the Eternal City in 1987. 'I went to Italy because it's where I was born. It's my country,' he explains. But Chinaglia says he still has 'a draw' to the States. He owns a house in Florida, which the family uses as a holiday home, and he frequently returns to New York where his mother and sister still live.

Chinaglia works in the media, behind and in front of the camera, and runs two television companies, Noi l'Immagine and Tele Euro 2000. He is now one of Italy's best-known football pundits. A man of strong opinions, Chinaglia is well suited to the world of football analysis and the re-emergence of Lazio as a genuine force in Italian football (the Romans won *Lo Scudetto* for a second time in 1999–2000) has improved his profile. He began commentating for TMC (*TeleMontecarlo*) before graduating to RAI (Radio Audizione Italiana), Italy's national broadcaster. 'It's my vocation. I work hard and people always want me as a commentator. Having been a player you try to predict what's going to happen. It's easy.'

Like so many of Italy's top players, he turned his back on the high-pressure world of coaching. 'Because I was owner of a club, I never had any thoughts of being a coach,' he says. 'Maybe I was never cut out for it.' He remains an idol for half of Rome, the symbol of Lazio's first, great triumph. Restaurants which are *laziale* let him eat free, and whenever he goes shopping he is stopped for autographs and pictures. 'People remember. It's nice to be recognised.'

The ex-striker has recently received two personal awards. Lazio celebrated their centenary in 1999 and in a poll organised by *Corriere dello Sport*, Chinaglia was voted the club's Player of the Century, ahead of the legendary Silvio Piola. 'He was the only Lazio player,' said Franco Dominici, a journalist on the *Corriere* since 1959 who voted for Chinaglia, 'who gave the team, before the 1990s, an authentic winning mentality. Without him, Lazio would never have won the championship.'

Nicola Pietrangeli, a former tennis player and Italy's number one from 1959–70, also chose 'Long John'. 'He was the flag of Lazio, he won the league title and he was a leader on and off the pitch. I have never known another player who attached himself to a club more than he did. During the year of the championship he was fundamental.'

The newspaper presented ten people with a list of every Lazio player since 1929–30, the season the modern Italian championship started, and from that list asked them to pick the club's greatest player. Apart from Dominici and Pietrangeli, those polled included former Lazio coach Dino Zoff, in charge of the Italian national team at the time; current Lazio president Sergio Cragnotti; former Lazio goalkeeper and coach Roberto Lovati; and Maurizio Maestrelli, one of the sons of championship-winning coach Tommaso Maestrelli. There were votes for Giuseppe Signori, the fair-haired forward who topped the *Serie A* goalscoring chart three times during the 1990s, Mario Frustalupi, the playmaker in the Lazio side of 1973–74, and Alessandro Nesta, the formidable stopper and captain of the present Lazio team. But it was *Giorgione* who was named *il giocatore del secolo* – Player of the Century.

'I would have given my vote to Piola but Giorgio won the championship,' explained Mario Pennacchia, a former journalist and press officer for the club. 'He was a true leader, a warrior, the man who gave the team character. He was Lazio through and through.'

Enrico Montesano, one of Italy's best-known comic actors and a lifelong Lazio fan, gave similar reasons for choosing the top scorer of 1973–74. 'There have been many strong players who have worn the sky-blue shirt, however Giorgio was the man who won the championship. He was a grandiose forward, an example of someone who attached himself to the colours of the club, a leader. And he had a heart that was truly Lazio.'

In 2000 Chinaglia was inducted into the US Soccer Hall of Fame. His photograph and biography being 'enshrined' in the Hall of Fame museum in Oneonta, three hours north of New York. Chinaglia also received a medal and gold ring from the US Soccer Federation. The Hall of Fame was launched in 1979 yet the NASL's most prolific goalscorer had to wait eleven years before he was finally recognised. 'Chinaglia has been overlooked,' says Will Lunn, director of the Hall of Fame. 'He wasn't very popular when he was with the Cosmos. Some people didn't like him as a person. He rubbed people up the wrong way. But look at the statistics and he's above Pelé.'

Chinaglia benefited from the new voting system to elect soccer greats into the Hall of Fame. Before 2000 the presidents of the various state associations – in effect, politicians – decided who would be a 'Hall of Famer'. That has been changed. Now the decisions rest with three former US national team coaches, three former US internationals and members of the Professional Soccer Reporters Association. Immediately they voted for Chinaglia. 'Franz Beckenbauer was the first Cosmos player to be inducted but maybe Giorgio should have been the first,' says Lunn. 'When it comes to achievement, Giorgio stands out. He was the best player in the NASL. He scored seven goals in a play-off game against Tulsa, which is pretty unnatural.'

Continues Lunn, 'Giorgio is highly regarded in the States as a player. The fact they voted for him shows how highly he performed. If you're in the Hall of Fame, you've made it. You become immortal.'